Chelsey

Chelsey

Chelsey Shannon

Health Communications, Inc.
Deerfield Beach, Florida

www.hcibooks.com

Library of Congress Cataloging-in-Publication Data

Shannon, Chelsey.
    Chelsey / Chelsey Shannon.
        p. cm.
    ISBN-13: 978-0-7573-1413-1
    ISBN-10: 0-7573-1413-9
    1. Shannon, Chelsey.   2. Teenage girls—United States—Biography.
  3. Teenage girls—United States—Psychology.   4. Bereavement in
  adolescence—United States.   5. Adolescence—United States.   I. Title.
  HQ798.S454A3 2009
  305.235—dc22

                                                      2009019607

Publisher: Health Communications, Inc.
                3201 S.W. 15th Street
                Deerfield Beach, FL 33442–8190

Cover design by Larissa Hise Henoch
Interior design and formatting by Lawna Patterson Oldfield

To my parents,
Amy and Blair Shannon

Contents

Part One

Part Two

Part One

Last Minutes of Peace

i climbed the hill

        walking toward

home, where i don't know

        a disaster

is waiting, one that i

        won't

wake up from, won't

        disappear

The Beginning

I'LL BEGIN AT THE BEGINNING. I was born to family who were overjoyed at my arrival. Deeply in love, my parents were a biracial couple—my father, Blair, was black, and my mother, Amy, white. My parents dated for eight years before they were married, and by that time, my mother's large, Catholic family had accepted my father as a surrogate brother and son. My parents worked well together, both as lovers and as business partners. In the years before I was born, my parents ran a comedy club in downtown Cincinnati called Aunt Maudie's.

I was conceived shortly after the tragic death of my Aunt Kim in a car accident; a joy to balance a sorrow. My father filmed my mother's cesarean section and my subsequent birth. As my tiny, slippery self emerged from my mother, all he could say, with the utmost reverence, was, "Oh, my God." The first time my mother held me, she wept quietly. In watching the tape today, I can almost feel what she must have felt at that moment: relief, exhaustion, joy, awe, gratitude, and overwhelming love.

After my birth, we moved to a growing suburb of Cincinnati, Ohio, called West Chester and built a red, brick house to live in. I remember exploring our budding home as it slowly emerged from the ground up, my parents planting a small garden in the front, selecting paint chips and carpet samples. Ours was one of the first homes in the area.

Though my mother initially continued her work as a secretary during my early childhood, she soon decided to stay home with me, as, back then, my father spent much of his time on the road, staying in various cities as he pursued his career in stand-up comedy and music. Though she missed having him at home, my mother supported my father's endeavors, recognizing his talent.

The first few years of my life went smoothly and safely. But things started to change by the time I reached kindergarten.

When I was five years old, my mother was diagnosed with an acute form of leukemia, a cancer of the blood. Before my young eyes, the life was drained from my once vivacious and lovely mother, her face becoming pale and gaunt, her ebony hair thinning before giving way to baldness. By the time I started first grade, my mother was hospital-bound. By October of 1998, she was gone. My father was out of town when she died but asked my relatives who were staying with me to wait to tell me so he could break the news. As soon as he arrived home, he led me outside to the front porch of our house, and we gazed up at the velvety night sky, which was studded with stars that shone like diamonds. Deep in my heart, I knew what was coming.

"See that big, bright star up there?" my father asked gently, kneeling so he was beside me. I nodded.

"That's Mommy."

My worry confirmed, I clung to my father, beginning to cry. Though, in some ways, I'd known that my mother wasn't going to make it, I was still devastated that one of the most important people in my small world was gone.

A few days later, as I sat among my first-grade classmates and listened to my teacher explain my family's tragedy in words and concepts we could understand, I began to feel my life would always be different from those of my classmates—not necessarily less happy or functional, but definitely unconventional.

The years that followed confirmed my suspicions. Despite being a fairly happy and conventional family following the dark period of grief after my mother's death, there were still subtle nuances that distinguished me and my father from others in our community. The chief difference lay in my father's occupation. My father had transcended the realm of dingy clubs and hotels and begun to perform on cruise ships. He deeply enjoyed what he did and was quite successful at it. His work, however, made it necessary for him to leave me, his only child, roughly two weeks out of every month so he could perform at sea. This fact certainly didn't fit the mold of a typical suburban childhood. Unlike my friends, I didn't always have a welcoming parent to walk home to, a supportive face in the audience of a concert or recital, or a ride home from the bus stop in the rain.

Even so, I had a fairly happy childhood and learned to adjust to my circumstances. While my father was away, I stayed with our neighbors, the Rouses, whose daughter, Holly, was only a year older than me. Because we were next-door neighbors, I was never far from my own home. By the end of my thirteenth year, I had established a reasonably simple rhythm to my life: dad gone, dad home, the Rouse's house, my own. But a week before my fourteenth birthday, my life was drastically uprooted.

In my relatively short time on earth, I have learned that life, among many other things, is fully capable of taking detours from the path we envision for ourselves. These detours can be pleasant or traumatic, minor or deeply altering—but we all experience them, and we all must learn to deal with them.

In my life, the detours took the form of the premature death of my parents. These circumstances have simultaneously been the most difficult and life-changing ones I've had to deal with. The early losses of my parents feverously spurred me on to a path of change, healing, and a deeper under-standing of myself. Though the grief at my parents' deaths—my father's in particular—seemed insurmountable at times, it also initiated my quest of discovering who I truly am.

Finding Out

THE DAY MY LIFE was altered irrevocably was an unsus-pecting cold and gray January day. At school, I coasted thoughtlessly through my biology, language arts, and pre-algebra classes, distracted by thoughts of the weekend and my father coming home from his latest trip—a trip on which he'd brought his girlfriend, Monique, along. My only cause for concern was my failure to reach my dad earlier that morning, since he had told me the previous night I would be able to call him before I headed to school.

However, by the end of the day, I was no longer worrying as I walked up the hill from my bus stop with the boy who lived down the street. We laughed, talking about nothing in particular. When we reached the top of the hill, he parted from me, and I said good-bye. As I turned toward my house, I registered the two cars in my driveway: my Aunt Chris's green one and my grandparents' gold one.

Confused, I headed down to the end of the cul-de-sac where my house sat. *Why are they here?* I wondered. I knew I was spending the weekend at my grandparents' house, but as far as I knew, they weren't supposed to pick me up until the following day. And even if they were picking me up early, why were *both* cars there?

Slight panic filled me. My mind automatically jumped to the worst conclusion: *Did someone die?* I frantically scanned the possibilities as I closed the distance between the house and me: maybe my grandma or grandpa died, or maybe a more distant relative.

Finally, I reached the house. My grandma opened the front door before I had a chance to reach for the knob. Her eyes were sad as I gazed into them. She said hello, her voice scarcely concealing melancholy.

Why is she looking at me that way . . . like she feels sorry for me? I wondered as she embraced me.

"Why are you guys here?" I asked politely as I could, walking down the hall into the kitchen. My grandpa was there, as well as my Aunt Chris, who was passionately sobbing.

God, no . . . what happened?

I opened my mouth to ask, but my aunt came to me instead, holding me by the shoulders. "Something terrible has happened," she kept repeating. It became her mantra, her prayer to protect us all from the truth.

Disarmed by the presence of both of my grandparents, I had little notion of what might have happened, and why my aunt, who scarcely ever cried, was so upset.

"*What?* What happened?" I asked, growing angrier and more anxious with each repetition.

"Now, you can scream or do whatever you want when I tell you this," she finally managed through her tears. I attempted to steel myself, but the truth was far beyond my naive notions of what the worst-case scenario could be.

"Your dad has been killed."

What?!

Instantly, I felt angry. I wanted desperately to strike my aunt for telling such a joke; it wasn't funny at all. I was filled with hate toward my relatives for coming to my house and disturbing my afternoon with such cruel mockery.

Dad's coming home tomorrow morning, I wanted to snap at them. *I don't know what you all think you're talking about.*

Even so, I felt the world around me begin to slip away, my vision swimming as lightness filled my head. I couldn't stand . . . I couldn't think. Part of me, somewhere, knew that it was true. Part of me knew there was no joke—that they were not lying.

I felt the color drain from my face, and my relatives led me to the couch. My aunt sat down beside me and began to tell me what little details she knew: "Attempted robbery . . . shot . . . last night . . ."

Her words scarcely pierced through my fog of defiance. I felt so *angry,* more so than I'd ever felt in my life. But something happened. As she listed the details of the horrible crime, some part of me realized she couldn't have just been making it all up on the spot. Why would she? I saw the tears in her eyes, and I knew she wasn't lying. Then I started to cry too.

Aftermath

THE EVENING THAT followed was the most hollow and bizarre of my life. My Aunt Chris, my grandparents, and I prepared to wait the evening out and were eventually joined by the Rouses and other neighbors. Though a kind gesture, the company didn't really help much, as no one knew what to say. Silence permeated the house as it never had before. Our spacious family room was full, but no one spoke. We all sat quietly, lost in our own thoughts, our own imaginings and dreads of the future.

A sense of somber anticipation had fallen over us all. Though no one would explicitly state it, I had the distinct feeling I wasn't the only one who thought that, maybe, this would still all be revealed as a joke. It was as if we were all hoping—some of us praying—that if we sat quietly enough, we would hear my father's car pull up and he would enter through the garage, laden with luggage and some crazy story explaining the horrible mix-up. We'd laugh and cry from relief, and everyone else would go home. It would just be me and him, and I'd be happier than I've ever been.

This didn't happen, of course. We ordered pizza that I couldn't eat. Meager attempts at conversation were made, but mostly, there was silence. Disbelief clouded my thoughts as grief threatened to take over my heart. I simply couldn't believe it to be true. Not yet, not all of me.

After all, everyone knew murder didn't happen in real life or to good people. Murder belonged in faraway countries where it couldn't bother us or safe within the confines of a movie or TV screen, where it could be ogled at from a safe-enough distance. Murder, I maintained, did not belong in my world. It was simply inappropriate, and it certainly had no place in ending my father's life.

So I wouldn't believe it. I humored my family and the people who visited, but inside I mocked them, called them fools, for surely this was just an elaborate joke being played on us all. And when a television crew from some heinous, new reality show jumped out from behind the corner, or my dad burst through the front door, full of apologies and humorous explanations, I would be the only one not caught off guard.

Convinced that the sooner I went to bed, the sooner I would wake up from the nightmare, I retired at around nine o'clock, Holly joining me soon after. It was a dreamless void of a sleep, precisely what I needed to forget all that had happened.

The next day, I woke up early, the rest of the house still steeped in slumber. I rose quietly, not wishing to wake Holly. In my head, hope gathered. I was certain the previous night was just a horrible mistake, and that if I followed the hallway from my room to his, I'd find him within, safe and sleeping in his bed. He'd have arrived in the middle of the night. He'd be tired but wouldn't mind that I'd woken him; he'd just be happy to see my face. He'd get up, and we'd eat pancakes together. It was Saturday, after all.

This was the scene I felt sure awaited me down the hall behind his closed bedroom door. With caution, careful not to step where the floor creaked, I followed the path of refuge as I'd done after numerous nightmares and on countless mornings. He'd be there, sound asleep, just like all the times before.

I turned the knob and opened the door. The bed wasn't just empty—it hadn't been touched. I could tell by the smoothness of the sheets, the position of the pillows. It just looked like my dad's bed on any other day when he was away. I don't think I've ever felt a disappointment so crushing.

My parents' bed was grand: king-size and comfortable. My father had slept on the left side, my mom on the right. After my mother died, my dad kept to the left side for years, as if saving the right for her, should she ever wish to reclaim it. Sometimes, when I missed her, I'd go and lie on the right side. After a few years, Dad had migrated to the center of the bed. Still, in my mind, my parents had their sides of the bed. I lay on the left side and sobbed. I buried my face in the pillow, anxious to absorb whatever essence of my dad lingered on the fabric.

It was only at this point that I truly allowed reality to burst through my protective web of denial and rage. As I lay on my father's bed, I wept, feeling the deepest sorrow I've ever felt, in sobs that are usually kept inside, sobs that are accompanied by wails and aching chests.

After a while, I tried to distract myself. Sobs still falling from my lips, I rose from the bed and quietly shut his door behind me. I went downstairs to attempt to eat something but failed again. My body simply rejected the food.

I then tried to watch *American Idol*, which my dad and I recorded each week and watched together. But I couldn't focus. I could barely hear the television. All I could think about were my own words to my father in an e-mail a few days earlier: "Don't worry. I won't watch *AI* without you." I turned off the television.

Still, there was nothing else I could do. The reality of the situation had literally taken over my mind. I thought I had known distraction before, but nothing compared to my total inability to consider anything else but my father and his death. All I wanted to do was talk to him. I dialed his cell phone number several times, hoping against hope that he would answer, but the calls just rolled straight to voice mail.

Rather blindly, I grabbed a notebook and returned to my father's room. I began to write him stream-of-consciousness letters, in which I reverted to being his clinging little girl, begging him to come home, to make the nightmare go away. Only when I wrote could I stop crying. I wrote for most of the day.

1/21/06

Dear Daddy,

This has to be a dream. Please, let it be a dream. I love you too much to lose you like this. How could anyone take you away from me, and everyone else who loved you? And so many people did, Daddy. Oh, God. How could I ever live without you?

You taught me so much. You were such a fascinating person. How could you leave like this, when no one was ready for you to?

I feel like I'll never be able to enjoy anything again, Daddy. I can't eat, I can't watch television, I can't talk to anyone. All I want to do is sleep, where I can feel nothing. When left alone with my thoughts, I am tormented, and I keep crying, Daddy.

Remember on the day of my concert, when I said, "I don't want you to die?" It was almost like a premonition, I suppose. I kept thinking of Les Misérables, the part where Valjean is dying too soon, leaving Cosette behind.

It is too soon, Daddy. I thought we had years and years together, and we would be the best of friends.

But I take some comfort in the fact that I got to talk to you beforehand and tell you that I love you. And I can only pray that you are watching me from heaven, with Mommy finally by your side, watching me and loving me together, as you never could before. Is heaven nice?

When Aunt Chris told me, I was so angry. I didn't believe her, and I thought I would faint.

Daddy, I'm so glad I have all your e-mails, and your notes and voice mails.

I feel so alone—so, so alone and so empty. If only you could send me a sign, telling me that you're okay and Mommy's okay too.

My eyes are swollen from crying.

I'm so glad we always said I love you, and that you signed the books you gave me. There is so much of you in everything I own, in the house. This way, I can never forget you. I never will, Daddy. I'm far too attached to you for that. I'll write more later. I love you with all my heart.

What Happened

THE REST OF THE weekend passed in bleakness. My friends came over, comforting words and homemade chocolates shaped like roses in tow. There was fierce, blunt Abby; kind, considerate Kelsey; altruistic, analytical Bridget; and empathetic, sensitive Holly. I felt almost sorry for them. This level of involvement far surpassed all expectations of friendship between young teenagers, even if they were my best friends. Nothing in their lives had equipped them to comfort a friend dealing with the murder of her father.

As we sat in my family room attempting to enjoy ourselves, I wondered what they would do when they got home. Would they sit down with their families? Eat dinner? Laugh together? It seemed so achingly probable—so *normal*—that I felt jealous of them and their ability to get up and leave my house when it became too much for them. They could simply call their parents and ask to be taken home. But this over-whelming reality was now my life.

Amid company, and me crying, writing, and rather list-lessly beginning a scrapbook, Monique, my father's girlfriend, returned from St. Thomas, deeply and understandably rat-tled. Monique had been with my father when he was killed and was able to share additional details of the tragedy, despite, I'm sure, a horrible sense of grief and shock.

One of Monique's first stops when she'd returned to Cincinnati had been my house. She immediately began cry-ing when I answered the door and she saw my face, embrac-ing me and apologizing over and over. Once she'd calmed down and settled in the family room, she sadly went into the details of my father's death.

As I already knew, the two of them had planned to spend the night at a hotel in St. Thomas after a weeklong cruise in the Bahamas. The next morning, they were to board a plane to Cincinnati and be home in time for the weekend. They'd had a pleasant enough day in St. Thomas before setting in at their hotel. Monique had had a bad feeling about the hotel and thought the one across the street gave off a much better vibe. However, the hotel they ended up in was cheaper, and they fig-ured it wouldn't make much difference for just one night.

Unfortunately, they were wrong. Slightly after eleven

o'clock that night—no more than an hour after I spoke to my father for the last time—a man entered their room while my dad and Monique slept, squeezing in through the sliding patio door they'd left slightly ajar to air out the room. My father awoke to the noise and rose from the bed, waking Monique as well. My father assumed the man had intentions of robbing them and told him to take whatever he wanted, so long as he didn't hurt anyone. Monique, nervous, began urging the man to go away, to not commit such a grievous crime that he would only regret. The man became agitated by Dad and Monique's words; likely he'd entered into the act assuming anyone in the room would remain asleep and he wouldn't have to deal with the reality of what he was doing. As he backed away, he shot blindly into the darkened room. The bullet hit my father in the chest.

Monique, understandably, began to panic. Dad, on the other hand, with his characteristic collectedness, sat down on the bed and picked up the hotel phone to call the front desk.

"'Call an ambulance,'" Monique told me he'd said with an amazing calm. "'I've been shot.'"

The help didn't arrive fast enough. My father—the man who had protected me, loved me, provided for me, and who I thought would always be there—sunk to the floor as the life drained from his body. Monique had knelt beside him as he died, had heard his final breath escape his lips, had seen his warm brown eyes close for the last time.

Miles away, I lay in my bed at the Rouses, totally unaware of what had just happened to my dad, and what would happen to me and my family as a consequence. Even though I was not there when my dad was murdered, as Monique told me the story, I could practically see the terrible scene unfold before me, and I felt a horrible ache in my own chest like the one my father must have felt in his as he died.

Back to School

MY ALARM BLARED at 6:15 AM on Monday morning, just as it had so many weekdays previously. I rolled from bed, mind fogged. As I attempted to focus on getting ready for school, my aunt materialized in my doorway.

"What are you doing?" she asked anxiously, still sounding somewhat groggy.

"Going to school," I replied matter-of-factly.

"But you're not ready!" she pleaded. "I think you should just stay home."

"No," I said calmly, but firmly. "I have to turn in a paper for my group."

That was true. I had spent the previous night completing the essay on *Les Misérables* my language arts group had assigned me. It wouldn't be late because of me. Somehow, in the midst of all the insanity and anguish that had been unleashed on me and my family, school was one of the only things I could think about. *I have to finish typing those questions. Isn't there a vocab test today? I didn't finish up that math homework.* The mundanity of it somehow comforted me.

"Plus, I want to gather any work I'll need to do," I added when she hesitated, but this was an excuse. Really, I just wanted to get out of the godforsaken house and escape from reality for a moment, to be swept away in the nameless, thoughtless current of students going from one class to the next. I wanted to be in control again, to be in a place where I always did well. School was my element—this strange place that was supposed to be home no longer was.

My aunt gave in when I made it clear I wouldn't be staying home, that I couldn't handle it. I set out toward the bus stop, the early morning chill familiarly nipping at my cheek. In my mind, it was my father, not my aunt, standing on the deck, waving good bye, calling out that he loved me and to have a great day. I could almost hear his voice caressing my ear.

At the bus stop, my friends were silent. They were boys, uncertain of what to say. They watched me, begging me to give them a clue. Finally, I cracked a wry but lame joke, breaking the silence. I knew they knew about my dad, either from the news or from one of the neighborhood mothers. They laughed uneasily, folding their arms across their chests. We didn't say anything else. The bus came. Another Monday morning.

The rest of the day wasn't quite so routine. My first destination, the band room, had never seemed so formidable. The thought of walking across the front of the room, in perfect view of dozens of classmates, made me quake.

My friends flanked me as we traveled the hall, anxious to offer any moral support they could, but their bodies might as well have been transparent for how exposed I felt. As we made our way down the hall, the usually flowing morning banter stilted and unnatural, I wanted to turn and run home, in spite of my earlier insistence on going to school. But this was my choice, and I knew I couldn't back out.

When we reached the band room, my friends dispersed to get their instruments and I walked alone to get my bassoon, attempting to look dignified and strong and collected. But I knew how pale my skin was, how limp my hair, how messy my outfit. I knew they would know as much as I did, the story having spread across newspapers and local news channels. My family's tragedy had been circulated and regurgitated throughout the community and beyond, before we'd even had a chance to digest it ourselves. My loss wasn't even mine to tell.

I felt my classmates' eyes appraise me with a mixture of pity and discomfort. Always a shy and awkward person, being the focus of such attention would have made me uneasy even before I'd become an orphan.

Identity

ALL MY LIFE, I'd been a fairly reserved person. Since my mother's death especially, I'd been a pensive, quiet child who required much prodding before I'd genuinely participate in a conversation. I tended to shy away from meeting new people and sometimes even from conversing with friends and family members I already knew.

Some of my shyness had dissipated by the time I reached junior high, and I had a tight circle of interesting friends as well as a broader spectrum of acquaintances. In spite of this progression, by seventh grade, my self-confidence was at an all-time low. Though I generally liked who I was as a person, issues with my appearance caused my opinion of myself to plummet. I saw myself as overweight and ugly. And as these beliefs festered, they bred new ones: *You're incapable. You're so fat. No one will ever ask you out.* Eventually, even though I'd always considered myself to be a bright, intelligent person, I began to believe I had nothing of consequence to say, and that no one really cared, anyway. I consistently preferred fading into the background. Presentations and other such occasions where attention was focused on me were a nightmare.

These insecurities, in addition to continuing to deal with the aftermath of my mother's death, my father's occupational situation, and some difficulties in my friendship with Holly, made for a difficult eighth-grade year even before my father's death. I felt I was a nuisance to everyone who had to take care of me aside from my father—the Rouses, my Aunt Chris, my grandparents. I was generally dissatisfied with life and felt blue most of the time. Eventually, such statements as *Things would be easier if you weren't around* began to appear in my litany of negative thoughts. As a result, my father started taking me to see a counselor.

On top of this dissatisfaction, I was also finding it difficult growing up as a biracial young woman in a predominantly white area. Race, as a notable component of identity and personal history, was always slightly confusing to me. The majority of my friends, neighbors, and teachers were white. My father and his family were African American.

Though at the time I was much closer to my mother's family than my father's, racial stereotypes confused me, and I was never quite sure who I did—or "should"—identify with. Though I fit within my community for the most part, there were times when the differences seemed to far outweigh any similarities, when the color of my skin seemed to differentiate me from everyone else.

If it hadn't been for my close relationship with my father, things would have been that much more difficult for me. In the weeks that followed my dad's death, I sometimes wondered whether his murder was meant to punish me for feeling so depressed about my life, when really, it hadn't been all that bad. Like some higher entity watched my petty misery and thought, *You think things are bad now? Well, let's see what you think of this.* But I knew that wasn't really true. I knew my circumstances were just a horrible misfortune.

Following his death, I found it hard to explain our relationship to others who were not familiar with it. How could you really describe afternoons wasted together playing video games and eating sandwiches, laughing and talking as if there was no one else we'd rather be with? Or bedtime stories and sweet goodnights that were my favorite part of the day? Or the day when my father asked me to gaze up into the navy October sky and told me my mother had died?

I can't express how happy I was when my father allowed me to keep two cats as pets, in spite of our allergies, or how proud I felt when he'd praise my latest accomplishment in school or music, or how safe I'd feel when he pulled me into a hug. There was no awkwardness between us, a teenage girl and her father, as is always portrayed in popular media: we hadn't grown apart. We had remained close even as I got older because, at one dark point, we'd been all each other had.

So when I attempt to describe my relationship with my dad, I simply say that he was my best friend. I could talk to him about anything. We got along very well as people, and enjoyed having intellectual and cultural conversations. We would introduce each other to new hobbies and interests and make each other see things in a different way. I always knew our relationship was special, despite the setbacks of my dad being a single parent and being away much of the time.

My father's partial absence put a strain on our relationship, of course. But in some ways, this propelled us to be even closer and forced us to maintain a basic connection, even when he was away. We'd frequently e-mail and call during the weeks when he was gone, and in this respect, I probably talked to my dad more than many kids my age talked to theirs, even if their fathers were home.

Of course, there was the constant concern that my dad

would miss something important in my life: band concerts, academic honors, and other such occasions. Though he tried his best to make it to everything, it simply wasn't always possible. The one day he refused to miss, however, was my birthday. Dad always made this day extremely special, giving me probably too many gifts. When I turned six, he even allowed me to have all my friends from school over for a sleepover. I relished celebrating my birthday because it reminded me of how special I was to my dad and how happy my parents had been to have me. Despite tradition, however, on my fourteenth birthday, a week after my dad had been killed, celebrating was the last thing I wanted to do.

Happy Birthday

IN THE WEEKS preceding my dad's death, we'd been making loose plans for my birthday. What I was most looking forward to was having dinner with my dad at the Macaroni Grill, my favorite restaurant at the time. So my family decided to hold my impromptu birthday celebration there. It was probably the largest birthday party I've ever had. We rented out the party room, and I was allowed to invite as many friends as I wanted. My whole family was in attendance, as well. As I laughed with my friends, opened their gifts, and enjoyed the food, it was almost carefree and pleasant enough to forget that my father's funeral was the next day.

Monique arrived toward the end of the party, concern etched in her expression, deepening the wrinkles of worry that had begun to line her face in the week since my dad's death. She pulled me aside.

"Me and your dad's family are on the way to the funeral home," she said. "Did you want to see him before they close the casket?"

This was obviously not a question I wished to encounter on my birthday—or at all. But it was there, and I was obligated to consider it.

I turned back toward my family and friends, some of whom were glancing back at me in slight worry, others not noticing me and carrying on with their conversations, light as they could be under these circumstances, and enjoying their food and wine. I saw my friends engage in silly banter, talking about him or her and what to do next. I saw Mike and Peri, Holly's parents, chatting with my own family. I saw my Aunt Trish and Aunt Erin, in from California, a rare sight for me. And I saw their smiles, much like my mother's, however wan. I saw my father's family: his sister, Carolyn, his brothers, Lester and Myron, his niece, Shaunda. I saw my Aunt Chris beside her boyfriend, Roger, laughing as she'd cried earlier that day, and her sons, my cousins, Nick and Andrew. I saw my grandparents, now having lost two daughters, a son, and a son-in-law, still breathing, still smiling, softly, as they were surrounded by their remaining progeny.

Around me, I saw life, however broken and saddened and fragile. And in my reverie, I became keenly aware of the life within us all—of the laughing, dancing, and joyful life that had once burned within my father. I knew it was gone now, extinguished far too soon. But I also knew it was that part of my dad I wanted to remember forever—not him lying motionless and mirthlessly in a casket, a mere shadow of who he really was.

I turned back to Monique.

"I don't think I want to. You guys can go ahead."

Monique voiced her support of my decision, gave me a hug, and left to say good bye to my father in her own way. I returned to my friends and enjoyed the rest of my party. The funeral would be the next day.

Toward the End of the Party

i'm told
that i either can

or cannot go to see

his body.

it is a hard decision:

to see his body for the last time,
cold and lifeless,
dark brown eyes once warm, blank

or

remember him as he was,
full of life
and love.

well.

i guess it's not such a hard decision
after all.

Getting Ready

THE NEXT MORNING, I was awakened earlier than
usual, not due to my alarm clock or natural course, but by
my Aunt Trish and Aunt Chris. They spoke to me in hushed
tones, under the impression that the gentle volume would

lull me from my slumber more effectively. Conversely, it annoyed me, only compelling me to roll onto my side and go back to sleep. Unfortunately, this would not stand. They managed to rouse me from my bed. I dressed quickly, my outfit entirely black, my face unusually pale and drawn, my curls artlessly pulled back.

Surprisingly, I had a healthy appetite, in spite of the unpalatable circumstances of the rest of the day. I ate a cheese omelet, a buttered piece of toast, and a small cup of orange juice. Shortly after I'd finished breakfast, our ride arrived.

As the others piled into the truck, I made my way to my father's study. While my fingers tried fruitlessly to fit the buttons of my black dress coat through their holes, my eyes searched the myriad shelves surrounding either side of my father's computer desk, all filled with expensive-looking hardback books, mostly biographies, with a few diet cookbooks and contemporary classic novels added for good measure.

It was a handsome collection. If a stranger had set eyes on the bookshelves, they would surmise, incorrectly, that my father had been an avid reader. Although my father was an intelligent man with a thirst for learning, he was more streetwise, with a minor in trivia. He could always answer any obscure popular culture question, and he knew how to get this or that done. Dad was always willing to help out.

I knew for a fact that he hardly ever read novels, and while he enjoyed biographies, he didn't read them very often. He once told me he had trouble concentrating on the text itself and preferred audio books. I wondered why any of that mattered now that he was dead.

As my hands finally managed to push one coat button through its hole, my eyes fell on a copy of *Roots* by Alex Haley. I remembered my father's words about the classic: *Never let that book go, Chels. It's a first edition—worth a lot of money. It was mine in high school.*

I temporarily abandoned the buttoning operation to gingerly pull the novel off the shelf. Flipping open the front cover, I found my father's name written in clean cursive with blue ink. I smiled as I thought of how drastically his handwriting had changed; back then, it was legible.

I set the book back in its place. My eyes filled with tears. There was so much of him in the house, in everything I now owned.

I thought of myself in a new light: a girl, newly fourteen, standing in her dead father's study, all in black, a single tear streaming down her cheek. A girl who couldn't button her coat. I was alone. My family told me again and again I was not, but without him, I was. I was no longer anyone's child; such a terrible change of status wasn't supposed to happen so early in life.

I closed my eyes, and quietly sang a song my dad had sung to me years earlier when I'd joined him for Father's Day on a cruise. I wept more at the sound of my voice—broken, weak, and small—as I sang a song that celebrated fathers and daughters, something I felt I could no longer be a part of.

Premonitions

THOUGH MY FATHER'S death took me so off guard as to propel me into a state of temporary disbelief, I can't say I was totally without premonition. The week preceding Dad and Monique's cruise, I found myself feeling unusually melancholy about my dad's impending departure. Though such emotions were familiar when I was younger, I had since overcome my separation anxiety and learned to deal with him being gone.

He'll be back in a week, I'd tell myself. *It's not that long.*

So I was slightly confused as to why, as he began to pack his bags once more, I felt the inexplicable impulse to beg him not to go, to do anything to keep him from leaving on his trip. I spent as much time with him that week as possible, feeling oddly nostalgic, even as I sat peacefully with him in the family room.

Why do I feel so sad? I wondered. *Nothing is wrong.*

The day before my dad left, I had a band concert that I was very excited about. It was the second year in a row that I'd participated in Honor Band, a region-wide ensemble that included only the finest players from all the schools in our Ohio district. The rehearsals were few but intensive, consisting of only one Friday evening and a full Saturday to prepare for the Sunday concert. Needless to say, I was proud of my contributions and efforts, and couldn't wait for my family to see me play clarinet with the band, especially because we were playing a medley from *West Side Story*, one of my dad's favorite musicals.

I had a large group of friends and family come to my concert, including my dad, Monique, Aunt Chris, my grandparents, Holly, and Holly's mother, Peri. After the concert, we went out to dinner at O'Charley's in celebration of my achievement as well as my impending birthday. Over the restaurant's signature sweet rolls and potato soup, I enjoyed a pleasant evening meal with my family and friends. We even told our waitress it was my birthday and were awarded with a small, chocolate birthday cake. Across the table from me, my father told stories that charmed everyone, and the rest of my family were being their usual, quirky selves. Yet, even then, I felt a sense of sorrow and unease as I looked into my father's smiling, brown face.

Once everyone had finished eating and my father had fallen silent as people broke off into smaller conversations, I rose from my seat at the table, walked to him, and sat down on his lap, a ritual I hadn't indulged in since I was a young child. He looked at me in confusion but didn't shoo me away, as he used to when I was younger.

Unable to quell the sadness within me, I wrapped my arms around him and lay my head on his shoulder.

"Daddy, I don't want you to die," I said quietly, pitifully.

Understandably, he was puzzled and slightly perturbed.

"Sweetheart, I don't want to die either." I straightened up and looked into his eyes. "Why would you say something like that?" he asked.

I hesitated. What was I supposed to say? That I had some sort of ominous inkling my dad would be taken from us? That the peace we were enjoying at the table would soon be shattered? What good would saying such a thing do?

I shrugged my shoulders.

Always aware of politeness in mixed company but not without concern, he said, "We'll talk about it later."

With a nod, I rose from his lap and returned to my seat. We never did talk about it later, but what good would it have done? He would have felt concerned, I would have felt worried, and he would have told me it was all in my head.

The Funeral

ON THE CAR RIDE TO Christ Emmanuel Christian Fellowship, a nondenominational parish in Cincinnati at which my Uncle Charles was a minister, I didn't speak. I played Pokémon on my Game Boy to distract myself from what was about to occur. We arrived at the church early, and my aunts and I filed into the first pew. I felt lost. In all the other funerals I'd attended—my mother's, my uncle's, and my Grandma Shannon's—my dad had always been right beside me, holding my hand and letting me cry into his shirt. Now, he was the one being buried, and I was all alone.

As the service drew nearer, the mourners began to arrive. I was struck by the immense crowd of people. An article in the *Cincinnati Enquirer* would later report that over two hundred people showed up. And all of them had formed a line in front of my pew to pay their respects to me and my family—many of them, even strangers, weeping as they pulled me into an embrace and told me how sorry they were.

There was my father's choral instructor from elementary school and his childhood friends. There were all my friends from West Chester, several of whom, in spite of a much anticipated band trip to Cleveland, had chosen to stay behind to support me. My friend, Amy, whom I'd known since first grade, and her mother, Lily, had flown in from Connecticut. My language arts teachers from both seventh and eighth grade, as well as my school counselor were there, and of course, the Rouses, my grandparents, Monique, my cousins from both sides of the family, my aunts from California, my Aunt Chris, my Uncle Lester and Uncle Myron, and my Aunt Carolyn, whose husband, Charles, was to officiate the service. Though my Aunt Pam and Aunt Kerry were unable to make it from California for the funeral, I knew they were with me in spirit. I felt almost overwhelmed by support and love, even in my sense of extreme isolation.

Once everyone's condolences had been offered and they took their seats, the service began. I found a surprising amount of comfort in my uncle's words, the soulful music and song, and the presence of those around me.

After the readings and a short sermon, people who had known my father well stood up in front of the crowd to give short testimonials, among them a man whom my father had known in his childhood and another longtime friend whom he'd known since high school. I was extremely touched to hear how my father had positively affected other people's lives.

When the testimonials were finished, it was my turn.

"And now we'll hear from Blair's daughter, Chelsey Shannon," my uncle announced to the congregation. My Aunt Chris immediately began weeping at the sound of my name, and I slowly rose from my seat to take my place at the podium, a letter I'd written to my father the previous day clasped in my hand. I took a moment to peruse the crowd before I began. It was easily the largest group of people I'd ever read to before, yet I didn't feel nervous.

"Hi, everyone," I said in an unpretentious, friendly voice. I cleared my throat as I struggled not to look down at the podium, hiding my face. With a small laugh at my behavior, I said, "My father was always telling me, hold your head up, you have nothing to be ashamed of." A chorus of affirmatives rang throughout the crowd. "So, I'm trying to work on that."

It was the oddest thing. In front of a two-hundred-person crowd, all eyes on me, eager to hear anything I had to say, I wasn't the slightest bit fearful or awkward or self-conscious. I felt full of a grace and ease that was entirely unfamiliar to me, especially under the circumstances, when I'd half-expected to break down and be unable to read my piece. But as I gazed into the crowd of people who had gathered to say good bye to my father, I felt only peace and a willingness to communicate what I had to say:

My dear father,

You were stolen from me, from all of us, in the most unfair of ways, and much too soon. We should have spent years and years more together.

Our house still stands, the world still turns, but my life will be forever altered and forever incomplete without your gentle, unwavering love. You taught me and everyone around you so much, and you could brighten one's day with only a few words.

I keep thinking to myself, Who would ever steal away a man that I, and so many others, held so close and dear? *The tears I've shed are countless. You were the strength in my life, the comfort, the warmth, the love; you were the guidance, the support, and I always did my best to make you proud, and I still will. For you made me proud every day, and you still do.*

You were the most gentle and thoughtful of men. Why you? Why us? What will I ever do without you, Daddy? It is so hard for me to accept that from this trip, you'll never return, that you'll never again hold me in your arms, never again laugh with me, never again tell me you love me.

As we lay you to rest, we remember all the countless precious memories we all shared with you, or else we remember what a hilarious, cheering, kind man you were. I promise you that you'll never be forgotten by anyone who knew you.

As for me, I'll remember you as the best father I ever could have asked for. My eternal wish is that we could have had more time on earth together, but at the same time, I look forward to someday coming home to your embrace once more.

I love you, I love you, I love you, and I know you will help me, and all of those who you loved, pull through this.

The church erupted into applause, and the congregation rose to its feet. I felt something within me change as I smiled softly back at the crowd. Maybe I *wasn't* so worthless. Maybe people *did* want to hear what I had to say. Maybe I wasn't incapable, or ugly, or stupid, as I'd begun to believe. As I descended from the podium to return to my seat, I carried myself with a certain pride and hope, feeling as though my father's spirit was traveling beside me. As untimely as it seemed, I somehow knew this was the beginning of many changes for me that would ultimately be for the better.

The rest of the funeral consisted of a slideshow put together by my cousin Shaunda. The pictures were set to my father singing from his CD, *Live at Sea*, which he'd released only a few weeks earlier. Images from my father's life drifted across the screen to the sound of his rich, baritone voice: my father singing his first solo at his childhood church at age five; my parents at their wedding; my dad holding a toddler version of me in front of autumn trees; and, most recently, photos of me, my father, and Monique at a production of *The Phantom of the Opera*, which we'd seen shortly after Christmas when it was touring in Cincinnati. Around me, my aunts had dissolved into tears as they gazed at a face they would never truly see again, the sense of loss magnified by the occasional appearance of my mother's image. I remained stoic, refusing to let myself cry, even as tears swam in my eyes and I had to bite my lip to prevent them from falling.

Looking back on it, I'm not exactly sure why I refused to let myself cry. I'd never believed that weeping indicated weakness and had been generally open about my feelings with the appropriate people. Most likely, I think the reason I remained emotionless was I believed if I cried, it would have meant he was really was gone. It would confirm everyone's horrific belief that these photographs and the tracks on the CD were the closest any of us would ever be to my father again. So I refrained from tears until we reached the cemetery.

It was remarkably warm and clear for a mid–January Cincinnati day. I was acutely reminded of something my father had said to Holly, Monique, and me on a recent day trip to the mountains of Kentucky. For some reason, we had been discussing funerals and how they always seemed to take place on rainy days. "It's not going to be raining at my funeral," my father had said with confidence. Of course, at the time, I had no way of knowing that his assertions would be so quickly proven true.

The large funeral crowd had shrunken by the time we reached the cemetery and gathered around a rectangular hole in the ground, the dirt freshly dug up beside it, the bright green cloth that's usually used for interment framing the hole. The coffin was beside the pit. I stared at it intently as a few final words were said and roses distributed to the immediate family, including me. Could this foreign, ever-oppressive wooden box, the kind that always struck me with the deepest sense of despair, really house my father's body? I half-believed it was empty or that they had the wrong man, that this was all just wrong.

My uncle stepped aside as the time came for us to approach the coffin and say a final good bye if we wished. I was encouraged to go first. I merely stepped up to the coffin—the closest I would ever be to my dad again—and didn't say or do anything. But I did break into tears, for the first time that day. I began to weep, hopelessly, in agony, as a voice gently but firmly whispered in my head, *He is gone*.

Tender arms pulled me away from the casket and held me as I watched my other family members say good bye through stormy tears. The image is rather blurred now, but what sticks out most clearly in my memory is my cousin Andrew, kneeling by my dad's casket, head slightly bowed, hand on the varnished wood as he said good bye to the uncle who wasn't his uncle by blood, but who he'd loved, like the rest of my family, just the same.

I wept as the casket was lowered into the ground, and then it was finished. The guests bid my family good-bye and uttered one more "I'm sorry" before dispersing into their respective vehicles and heading home. My dad's side of the family had rented out a hall for a reception, and many people joined us, but I had no appetite. I drifted through the rest of the day on autopilot, taking a bath in my parents' queen-size bathtub and reading condolence cards later in the evening before going out to eat with my friends Lily, Amy, Holly, and Jessica. I don't actually remember getting ready for bed that evening, but that's likely only because the oblivion that greeted me was so complete and welcomed.

Coping

THE DAYS FOLLOWING my dad's funeral were comprised of grieving his loss, dealing with the details of his murder, and attempting to rebuild my perception of "normal." Amid the isolation and despair, I had to go through the comparatively simple, yet emotionally taxing process of adjusting to my Aunt Chris's assumption of guardianship over me. I spent most of my time at home alone, unable to deal with the fact that, though I was still in the same house, my dad no longer lived in it with me and never would again.

Even so, had I not been allowed to remain in my house, I likely would have crumbled. Though it was merely a compilation of rooms filled with furniture and things, I took enormous comfort from remaining in the environment I'd inhabited for most of my life. In my mind, it seemed almost as though the house was the sole remainder of my immediate family. I knew it intimately: where the floor creaked when pressure was applied, the history of the color of its walls, which remote controls served which functions, where certain kitchen utensils lived.

My aunt's sons, Nick and Andrew, moved into the house with me temporarily so others would be there on the occasions when my aunt was unable or too tired to make the thirty-to-forty-minute commute from her job to my house. Though I cruised through those bleak days with a relative detachment and lack of involvement, my aunt understandably struggled to be present in West Chester as well as keep up her own condo in Colerain, where my grandparents also resided. Between acting as my caregiver, keeping her job, taking care of her horse, and dealing with her own feelings of loss, my aunt likely had the most stressful time of us all.

The days were relatively quiet and full of melancholy. I attended school every day, though there were times when I was overwhelmed by the comparative triviality of eighth grade. Sometimes, I'd opt to visit my school counselor over being frustrated in pre-algebra or literature circles in language arts. I began to eat lunch in my English teacher's, Mrs. Falato's, room. Sometimes, I'd only attend half a day, having my cousin Nick pick me up and take me home to rest.

By February, I had sunk into a quiet state of depression, attempting to deal with the crushing reality that my dad wouldn't be coming back. One night, I had a dream that brought me incredible solace. I was in my dad's room, and it was spring outside. I looked out to see a green van pull into my driveway. Though I didn't recognize the car, I was filled with elation at the sight of it. I saw my dad, wearing sunglasses, step out, along with a woman who also seemed familiar. I ran to the front door of the house to let them in, throwing it open. Dad was standing there, with the woman and many others who had exited the car with him. When I jumped into his arms, I woke up.

As I sat up in my bed, I breathed heavily as if I had really been running. Though the dream had been extremely abbreviated, I felt joyous as I looked back on it. I hadn't dreamt of my father since his death, and I'd found immense comfort and joy in the dream, almost as if it were a message from him, telling me he was okay and he was here.

I rose from bed happier than I'd felt in weeks and went downstairs into the kitchen, where my Aunt Chris was already eating. Grinning freely, I told her about the dream and how happy I'd felt. I was pleased when she shared my suspicion that it was more than just a simple nighttime reverie.

"Chels, remember after your mom died and I asked you if you had any dreams about her, and you said you did?"

I nodded. I remembered the dream well: my mother, as an angel, yet still bald from her chemotherapy, appearing to Holly and me. Only I could see her. My mother told me she was okay, that I didn't need to worry. I'd had a similar feeling of relief and gratitude back then.

"In my grief support group I went to after your mom died, they told us that the kids sometimes get messages, usually dreams, from whoever died, telling them everything is okay. That's why I was so excited to hear your mom had given you a dream. And now your dad has," she explained.

"Yeah. I'm really glad."

"And it's on the one-month anniversary too."

I hadn't realized it until she said it, but sure enough, when

I looked at the calendar, it read Sunday, February 19th. My dad never failed to honor a special occasion

Nick, Andrew, and I tended to relax when we were home together, playing GameCube and watching television shows and movies. I felt bad doing so little when my aunt was constantly on the go, but I honestly didn't feel I could handle any more. In addition to consistently vegging out, I threw myself into art of all forms, spending hours singing while accompanying myself on the keyboard, practicing my violin and bassoon, writing poetry, and sketching. I even composed a short melody on the piano, a feat I had never attempted before.

Once the weather grew warmer, I took to going on long bike rides around the neighborhood. I'd ride aimlessly, aware only of the burn in my muscles as I pumped up a hill, the cool breeze against my face as I glided down another. My neighborhood was essentially a long, circuitous route. I could go as far as I wished and essentially wind up back in the same place.

In the early spring, Monique and I joined a community theater production of *The Music Man*, one of my father's favorite shows. Though I was merely cast as a townsperson, I took pride in the fact that I was trying something new and totally outside my comfort zone. Before my father's death, participating in a theatrical production, no matter how minimally, would have been out of the question for me, in spite of my love of musicals and interest in theater. I would have hated the idea of standing onstage for all to see, my awkwardness on display. But after the funeral and reading my eulogy for my dad, community theater seemed to be no large feat—it was even an enjoyable project to undertake.

In truth, I enjoyed being a part of the musical more than I'd thought I would. I made friends with a few of the other "townspeople" who were my age, and when we weren't onstage singing and dancing to cheerful songs, we'd laugh and chat in the back, applying over-the-top stage makeup and attempting to harmonize. After months of rehearsals, we put on our production in an outdoor amphitheater in the park, and to the tune of "Seventy-Six Trombones" and "Wells Fargo Wagon," I watched winter slowly melt into spring and the time following my father's death evolve from days into weeks.

Spending so much time producing art and riding my bike served as a much-needed escape for me. I didn't hide from my problems—to do so would have been impossible—but there were times when I required a break. When I did things like methodically teach myself to play the keyboard or spend hours sketching family photographs, I was able to focus on creating something, rather than on what had been taken away from me.

Writing became a major refuge, the outlet into which I

poured all my emotions of fear, depression, and the occasional dash of anger. Although writing had ceased to be a primary pursuit of mine since grade school—when I was wont to begin a plethora of short stories but finish very few of them—I once again started writing journal entries, personal essays, and poetry. I was surprised to see writing resurface, especially in such an important capacity, but I was pleased. There was something very satisfying about seeing my thoughts and feelings crystallized onto paper. I wrote frequently, always attempting to refine my technique at conveying my emotions through words.

The Last Time

THE LAST TIME I saw my dad alive was in our kitchen, the night before he and Monique left for their cruise. I was in my pajamas and had gone downstairs to say goodnight before watching a movie with Holly, who was spending the night. My dad was on the phone, leaning his elbows against the counter as he often did. His itinerary for the forthcoming trip was on the kitchen island, as usual. Monique was also there, getting last-minute things together before retiring for the night.

I folded my arms around my dad as he wrapped up his conversation, resting my head on his shoulder. Tears sprang to my eyes for reasons entirely unbeknownst to me. My feelings of anxiety and dread at the impending separation bubbled over, and I felt as though I would never hug my dad again. I cried quietly so he didn't notice.

Wordlessly, Monique extracted her disposable camera from her purse and snapped a shot of this final embrace. At the time, I found myself mildly quizzical but didn't object. Later, when she presented me with two copies of the picture, I felt a deep gratitude for her intuitiveness.

I wiped the tears from my eyes as my dad hung up the phone. He turned to me and issued his usual going-away spiel: feed the cats, clean out the litter box, straighten up the kitchen, return his e-mails. I nodded along, not really listening, the sense of imbalance lodged in my breast. *Do I bring up my fears again or go with the flow?* I opted for the latter, not wanting to disturb him, especially not in Monique's presence. Instead, I agreed to his instructions, pushing my unease far away as I hugged and kissed him good-bye. As I walked up the stairs toward my bedroom, I had the distinct impression of leaving something I loved for the last time.

Once my dad and Monique had gone, I mostly forgot my earlier feelings of dread and fear. The week passed by in a completely normal fashion: on Monday I was off school for Martin Luther King Day, and the rest of the week was the usual mixture of school, homework, and music.

The last time I talked to my father was Thursday evening, right before I went to bed. He was in St. Thomas, in the hotel room where, a few hours later, he would die. Our conversation was commonplace. He said he'd call in the morning and that he and Monique would be back on Saturday. Distracted by what I was doing on the computer, I only half-listened to him, having no idea this would be our last conversation, in spite of my earlier premonitions. I tuned in for the end of the conversation, however, as we exchanged I love yous and said good-bye. I hung up the phone, closing any mortal connection between my dad and me.

Flying

When I was younger I was never afraid to fly.
With Dad sitting beside me,
I was confident that we would arrive safely—
in fact, no other possibility ever crossed my mind
and if we hit a patch of turbulence,
I'd cling to his arm for a moment
and I would be safe

and it would be over
and we would be fine.

Now,
I act brave,
like flying doesn't bother me,
when in truth,
it does a bit.
Gazing out the window
so far from the security
of ground and of him
I feel unstable, baseless
and when we hit a patch of turbulence,
I have no arm to cling to,
just false bravado
and broken reassurances.

Religion

For many kids in my school, eighth grade meant confir-mation into the Catholic faith. And I was one of the many about to begin the process of confirmation, despite my tumultuous relationship with the church.

My mother's side of the family was devoutly Catholic, and

before my mother's death, my mom and I regularly attended church. I absorbed the Catholic doctrine eagerly in childish wonder, even without really understanding what it all meant. I found the idea of God comforting and the concept of Jesus wonderful and generous. I said my prayers every night and set about to be as holy as possible. Until my mother fell ill.

When she was sick and after she died, my dad and I stopped attending church. I stopped praying at night. This wasn't specifically because I felt any anger at any God or because I felt particularly hopeless; rather, my mind was just consumed with other things, and I simply forgot about what used to be a sacred ritual of mine. Sometimes, in the dark days following my mother's death, I blamed myself for what happened.

Maybe if I'd prayed for her, I had thought, *she would have made it*. But such self-accusations were halfhearted. Somewhere, I already felt that nothing I could have done would have made a difference. I was even anticipating, in a sad way, my mother's death. When she'd grown quite ill, I drew her a picture of clouds and pearly gates that read "Welcome to Heaven." I don't know how she felt about that—if she felt hurt that all her efforts to stay alive were going to waste in the face of my muted acceptance or relieved for my silent blessing telling her it was okay to let go.

When she died, I did believe she went to heaven. And after I had the dream in which she appeared to me as an angel, the strength of those beliefs doubled. My mother, I steadfastly maintained, was an angel in heaven, watching over me.

It wasn't until I was ten years old that I began to question the Catholic doctrine. After my dad pulled through his depression following my mother's death and had gotten into the swing of being a single parent, we'd resumed attending mass. Not a Catholic himself, my father wanted to respect my mother's wishes of raising me in the faith. But the older I grew, the more I began to wonder if this was the right faith for me. Though I didn't disagree with any specific Catholic doctrine, I found it to be a very conservative faith socially, and this didn't sit well with me. My lack of agreement with Catholic positions on birth control, abortion, and homosexuality led me to research the faith, and in turn, others. When my father died, I was at a precipice of some great shift in my spirituality, just beginning to really examine what I believed in and what I did not. Interestingly though, by this time, I'd also resumed my nightly prayers, especially when Dad was away. During each trip, I asked God to bring him safely home.

When my dad died, I clung to the religious beliefs I'd been taught since childhood, praying even more regularly, thinking to myself that God was keeping him safe now, that God was watching over my family and me. I don't know if I truly believed this or if I just needed something bigger to believe in at a time when I felt so small and helpless. Either way, I'm glad I had it at the time.

But though I took comfort in the idea of God, I still wasn't feeling very warm toward the Catholic faith. Dad had started me on the path to confirmation before he died, and my Aunt Chris, a devout Catholic and my confirmation sponsor, wasn't about to let the matter fall by the wayside. So, following the initial shock of the tragedy, I resumed attending the bimonthly, Sunday night confirmation meetings. The meetings felt like a social event, much diluted by the presence of chaperones and discussions about God. So many people from my grade were going through the confirmation process that I would have felt odd *not* attending.

My aunt asked me if I wanted to postpone confirmation until the following year, when I might be in a better place to consider my spiritual allegiance. The way I saw it, though, it was simply now or later, and better to do it now, in the presence of those whose company I enjoyed. My friends Bridget, Abby, and Kelsey, as well as a few other acquaintances from school, were never far from my side in all matters confirmation-related. And though I'm not proud of it now, I coasted through what was supposed to be a devotional, intentional process with apathy, along with a small seed of resentment.

Despite of my lack of commitment, I did receive an extremely precious gift through confirmation that I never would have otherwise. It was definitely the only occurrence in my life that I'll ever consider a miracle.

In April, the month before our confirmation ceremony, it was announced we would all be receiving letters of encouragement from our respective parents and sponsors. I thought it was a nice idea, but I didn't feel particularly excited, assuming I would only be receiving a note from my aunt. But when two envelopes were delivered to my hands, I knew from my father's trademark messy script on the front of one of them that I was mistaken. My pulse elevated as I fought to suppress the joy that filled my heart, knowing that if I expressed all the happiness I was feeling, I would burst into tears. I sat in the pew alone, ripping the envelope open with simultaneous eagerness and extreme care.

The card depicted a beautiful black woman on the front reading, "Never forget how awesome you are." The inside of the card read, *"Dear Chelsey, as you travel this journey never forget: Believe in yourself and have faith that the power within you can make your life whatever you want it to be. All my love, Daddy."*

Also enclosed in the card was a loose sheet of paper filled with his near illegible, sacred script:

1/8/06

My dearest Peanut,

My love for you is unending, and you continue to amaze me with your musical talents and ability for expressive writing. Both are a direct reflection of your emotional maturity, and both are great. Your zeal for the things you love is worthy of envy. I know the parent is to set the example for the child, and I hope I do, but in many ways you teach me so much. For these reasons and many more I am proud of you, and I know your mother would be too.

I love you without bounds!
Daddy

I savored the miracle of each word of praise and encouragement, knowing these were the final words from my dad I would carry with me for the rest of my days, a father's last words of love to a daughter in lieu of the proper good-bye that had been stolen from us all.

I attempted to read slowly, but it was impossible not to let my eyes race onward, absorbing every word he'd said. By the time I reached the end of the letter, quiet tears had sprung from my eyes, running down my cheeks and gathering at my chin. My friends came to my side, and I showed them the letter.

"My dad wrote this!" I said in quiet amazement, not caring that everyone was seeing me cry. I couldn't believe the magnitude of this miracle, a final surprise and parting gift. I could never have imagined such a treasure could come from something I'd been so unwilling to do.

My issues with religion were temporarily dropped, and I went on to be confirmed with the rest of my friends in May. The ceremony didn't mean as much to me as perhaps it should have, but it made my aunt happy, as well as, I imagined, my parents.

Perspective

UNFORTUNATELY, RELIGION wasn't the only thing my Aunt Chris and I didn't see eye-to-eye on. Whereas my relationship with my father had been one of easy harmony and accord, my aunt and I occasionally butted heads. It wasn't that I disliked her—in fact, I loved her very much. She was one of the adults in my life who I found to be extremely responsible and unselfish. However, our communication styles differed, and we held distinctly separate interests. Whereas I was interested in art and literature, my aunt was into the outdoors and horses. It wasn't that we didn't make attempts to connect. It just didn't always work out when we did.

Chiefly, though, after my aunt became my legal guardian, I began pushing her away simply because she was not my father. Conversation wasn't as easy between my aunt and me. She didn't pack my lunches the same way. She didn't give the same hugs or laugh at the same things. And though I knew perfectly well that none of this was her fault, I couldn't help but disengage, even becoming short with her, despite how much I knew it hurt her.

I've always seen my Aunt Chris as a very dutiful person. She essentially took charge of the situation after my dad died, making tough decisions and stepping up to the plate at times when others couldn't. Even in the midst of grieving her brother-in-law, she was able to take care of me. Maybe I pushed her away because I knew she would always be there.

Aunt Chris continued to take me to see Donna, the counselor I'd been seeing since before my dad's death. In the last fifteen minutes of each session, Donna would invite my aunt into the room, and the three of us would have a check-in. These were often uncomfortable conversations for me. My aunt would allude to dissatisfaction with my behavior or her own emotional turmoil, and I would squirm in my seat. I didn't like facing the fact that Aunt Chris, who had always been so strong, was having troubles, too, and that they were partially my doing.

One counseling session in particular stands out in my mind. For some reason, my aunt asked her son, Nick, to drive us to the therapist. As usual, Aunt Chris came in during the last portion of the session, while Nick remained in the waiting room. We assumed our usual dialogue, and my aunt began to talk about the stress of maintaining both my house and her condo while still going to work and making sure I was taken care of, all on top of dealing with the loss of my father.

The therapist, Donna, said simply, "This is very hard for you."

My aunt nodded curtly, her voice adopting the matter-of-fact hardness it did when she was attempting to remain unemotional. "Yes. Yes, it is." Then she started crying. Then she started sobbing. It was as if Donna's simple words had opened the floodgates to the pain within my aunt—someone was finally noticing that she, too, was suffering, even if only in silence. Though she rarely cried in front of the rest of us, it didn't mean she never cried.

My aunt continued to sob through the rest of the session and the car ride home. Nick was stoic in the driver's seat, and I was lying prostrate in the back, facing away from the front. Neither of us said anything or tried to comfort her. We both realized this was something that needed to happen.

After this incident, I attempted to cultivate a stronger sense of empathy for my aunt, reminding myself when I felt the urge to snap at her or push her away, that she had feelings remarkably similar to mine.

Leaving Home

IN THE LATE SPRING, my Aunt Trish flew in for an extended visit from California. Though I loved all of my aunts dearly, I was probably the closest to my Aunt Trish. We'd enjoyed a special emotional connection since my childhood, and I was very pleased for her to visit. It was actually a test-run of sorts, as she was considering moving back to Ohio to live with me. For a month, she lived in my house, temporarily relieving Aunt Chris of some of her stress. At that point, Aunt Trish's nurturing disposition was just what I needed.

But Aunt Trish was also keen on stripping down the house, removing memories from it that were becoming too painful. With the question of moving increasingly in the air, she began the process of taking down pictures and packing away miscellaneous bric-a-brac. Rather than feeling angry, I felt gently saddened, the increasing lack of discernable warmth and character in the house matching my growing feelings toward it. I loved my house, but without my father, it just wasn't the same. It had become a stranger's home even before my aunt removed the pictures. By late spring, it became clear that I would be moving out of the house I'd lived in for most of my life. My father hadn't been faithful with paying off the mortgage, and my aunt's income was not ample enough to make up for his mistakes and support the two of us. Though I knew moving was a practical and, in some ways, healthy choice, the idea of leaving my home was very hard to bear.

One of the most difficult things, however, was unpacking my father's suitcase. The last suitcase he ever packed had been shipped to the house long ago, placed beside his bed, and shut away. His room had remained my refuge in the months following his death, and when I lay in his bed or holed myself up in his spacious closet to get away from it all, I would sometimes consider going through the suitcase. But the prospect was too painful, even though I knew it would have to be done eventually.

One Saturday morning, my Aunt Trish and I sat in the hallway outside his bedroom door and unzipped the black bag I'd been avoiding for so long. When she opened the lid, my father's gentle scent permeated the air, and tears sprang to my eyes. As I unfolded the T-shirts and unpacked his toiletries, I wondered what my father had been thinking as he'd packed his things for the final time: *Was he anxious to come home? Weary after a day of sightseeing? Excited to see me again?* I would never know.

With my Aunt Trish's gentle guidance, much of the house was packed away without incident. The most difficult part came when, one day, Nick was helping me pack up my room. As I sat motionless on my bed, Nick would hold up this object or that—an article of clothing, a knickknack, a book— and ask me "Pack or leave?" With one-word responses or a curt nod of the head, I watched my belongings—this small cell of my life—be pared down so they could fit into a few cardboard boxes and be carted across town to my aunt's condo until concrete plans could be made.

After a while, I asked Nick if we could take a break. He nodded.

"This is hard," he said simply.

I nodded back, trying my hardest not to cry, but I scampered from the room as tears began to roll down my cheeks.

It *was* hard. Though moving was certainly a part of everyone's life at some point, this moving was different. I wasn't one hundred percent sure where I was going, who I was going to live with, or even what school I'd be attending. With this moving, there wasn't even a semblance of certainty.

Toward the end of her visit, my Aunt Trish told me something I'd already realized: she wouldn't be moving back to Ohio. This disappointed me deeply, but I acted callous to protect myself. Even so, she invited me to stay with her in California during the summer, and perhaps consider moving out west with her. I agreed to visit, not making any promises about moving.

The rest of the school year was shaped around preparing for my visit to California. During my looming sojourn out west, I knew my family would finish packing up the house and move all my belongings to my aunt's house across town. When I came back—if I chose to come back—it was clear that I would be returning to the condo, not my house in West Chester.

Needless to say, melancholy permeated the final days before my trip, in spite of the sultry promise of summer. I became acutely aware of how I spent my final days in my house, not wanting to squander a second spent within the red brick walls. I'd stay up very late at night, anxious to absorb whatever bit of the house I could. One night, after a productive day of packing up my room, my bed was strewn with an assortment of belongings, and I ended up sleeping with a blanket on the floor.

On the last night at my house, I grabbed a pen and a flashlight and sat inside my now-empty closet, the secluded cell of my room I'd disappeared into when I'd needed a quick escape from reality. On the sidewall of the closet, near the bottom, I wrote the following inscription:

This is Chelsey's room, now and always.

Then, I turned off my light and went to bed, ready as I'd ever be to venture out into the world, away from my house, my dad, and the life I'd known so well.

Part Two

Sojourning

I FELT UNUSUALLY LIGHT and free on the plane to California. I'd only packed clothes that would carry me through a few weeks' stay, along with a few recreational essentials. Everything else had been left in the house to be boxed up and moved by my family, either to a storage space or to my aunt's condo. I looked forward to seeing my Aunt Trish again, as well as my Aunt Kerry and Aunt Erin, who I hadn't seen since the winter.

Aunt Chris and her boyfriend, Roger, were accompanying me on the flight, but after a few days at my Aunt Trish's, they would be assuming their own path to a more northern part of California to visit Roger's sister. For my part, I had mixed feelings about this vacation, which had the possibility of becoming a long-term move. Part of me was deeply grateful for the chance to escape Ohio and focus on my own healing rather than stewing in the maelstrom of depression. I believed the dry California heat and salty, forgiving ocean could help me become attuned to emotions other than grief once again, could breathe new life into a life turned stale by tragedy. Another part of me, however, was reluctant. I knew that when—*if*—I returned to Ohio, everything would be difficult. My house would no longer be mine, and I would be living with my Aunt Chris. I wouldn't attend my old school anymore. The Ohio I'd known for the first fourteen years of my life would be entirely changed. As I gazed out the window of the plane, I wondered how I could miss home since I didn't even know where home was.

We flew into the Santa Barbara Municipal Airport as the sun sank below the horizon and the western sky was being painted a dusky palate of purples and grays. My Aunt Trish and her husband Michael greeted us at the airport. We all piled into their car, exhausted yet talkative, and drove off into the mountains as the moon rose overhead. I had never been to this part of California before. To me, California was a rather pedestrian state, atypical only in its pronounced commercialism and abundance of beaches. But this was a California I was unfamiliar with: mountains higher than I could imagine, coated with sparse, reedy trees and separated by seemingly depthless valleys. We drove on thin, serpentine roads that hugged the mountainside for dear life.

Along the road, my aunt explained the part of town she was living in, a community known as Santa Ynez in the town of Los Olivos. She and her husband Michael were acting as tenants for a wealthy woman's property while she was away, tending to her horses and dogs, as well as working on renovating the house. The house itself was part of a gated development set in a largely undisturbed California mountainside. The area was secluded, peaceful, and calm.

When we finally passed through the gates of the neighborhood and pulled up to the house, I felt a uniqueness around me. The air was so clean as to almost seem liquid, perfumed slightly by the scent of desert. The moon was brilliantly white, as if bleached clean by the clarity of the air framing it. The stars twinkled with a dazzling effect I'd never before experienced. The vegetation surrounding the area, however sparse, truly seemed to be salient, breathing with the earth, emitting clear oxygen to be absorbed by our lungs.

The next morning, I found a similar sense of comfort and solace in my surroundings, though they themselves had done a veritable about-face: The sun was shining, the air dry and warm, the sky gently littered with cirrus clouds. Birds sang cheerfully as a gentle breeze stirred the sparse foliage.

I could stay here for a while, I thought to myself noncommittally as I joined my family for breakfast. And I did. After my Aunt Chris and Roger continued on their trip up north, I stayed with Aunt Trish and Michael, slowing getting to know Santa Ynez and its neighbor, Los Olivos. I found ample time to rest, write, read, and sleep, which had been my Aunt Trish's intention. The house behind the gate, set discretely in the woods, was a retreat, a hidden oasis of peace that I bathed in without hesitation. The only Internet there was dial-up, and I rarely bothered with it; there was no cell phone signal from the house. It was a change for me, who, up until that time, frequented MySpace and was usually texting someone or another. But in California, I was forced to be still and quiet with my own thoughts.

Healing

MY TRANQUIL SURROUNDINGS didn't always mean peace for me, though. There were times when I felt consumed by depression or uncertainty for my future, and I'd retreat to my bedroom to write or cry. I had plenty of time for reflection; I ended up writing a collection of twenty-five poems that told the story of my father's death, as well as several other individual poems and personal essays.

My Aunt Trish gave me space when I needed it and an empathic ear when I felt like talking. We'd always had a special relationship, but this trip solidified our bond. We'd spend time together talking, cooking, and running errands. For the first time in a long time, I was unconcerned with such trivial matters as homework assignments and cleaning my room, and was able to focus on more substantial things.

One of the most special things I did during my stay in California was visit a certain beach. I'd been to the ocean plenty of times in the past, having often accompanied my father on cruises, as well as visiting California before. I was always intrigued by how unique each beach was—how the mood, temperature of the water, and texture of the sand differed. One morning, my aunt told me we'd be going to a special beach that few people knew about. We packed snacks, sandwiches, and drinks for the day and set off on the two-hour drive. Unlike most of the beaches I'd visited, this one wasn't advertised and didn't attract large numbers of families. The path to this beach was flanked by mountains and seemed to go on and on. We didn't speak much in the car. My aunt focused on driving, and I gazed out the window in silent reverie.

When we finally arrived, I was anxious to see what all the

fuss was about. The beach was unlike any I'd ever been to before. There were only about ten other beachgoers to be found. Oddly, though it was warm, the sun was blocked out by clouds, and a cool wind was blowing. We set up camp, pinning a large beach towel down at the corners with our picnic basket and shoes, before I approached the water's edge and tested it.

As I slowly waded into the freezing water, I couldn't help but laugh at myself. No matter how unpleasant, it was nearly impossible for me to visit a beach without going into the water. I suppose oceans had some personal significance for me and always would. My father had worked on the ocean, often sending me gorgeous photos of the different beaches he visited or the sun setting on a horizon made entirely of waves. When I went with him on cruises, I'd take walks around the ship and lean against the railing of the deck, breathing in the moist, salty sea air. While the rocking of the ship at night made some people nervous or nauseous, I found it relaxing, like a mother gently rocking her child to sleep, and even after I returned to stable land, I would imagine the ground moving for a few days.

The sea fascinated me with its mysterious depth and power. It was one of the few places humanity hadn't entirely explored—one couldn't rattle off a complete list of facts about it without hesitation. This impressed me. Any place that had resisted the inquisitiveness—and arrogance—of humans deserved respect in my book. I loved stories about the ocean, from real tragedies like the sinking of the RMS Titanic, to strange phenomena like the Bermuda Triangle.

Visiting the sea had always felt like a homecoming to me. I'd often spend time finding a small relic of it that I could take home: a shell, stone, or sample of sand. Occasions where I could swim in the ocean were very special, almost sacred, particularly because I lived in a landlocked state. I was blessed in this respect by having family in seaside California and a father who'd worked so closely with the sea.

As I waded into the freezing water, goose bumps exploding on my skin, I turned around and waved to my Aunt Trish, who was reclining on the beach towel. Turning and attempting to gather courage to get my head in the water, I remembered the first time I'd visited a beach with my Aunt Trish.

Not long after my mother died, my father sent me to California to visit with my various aunts; I was about six years old. Aunt Trish took me to the Santa Monica Pier one day, and I was eager to take a quick dip, even though, at the time, the vastness of the ocean scared me, as it does most kids. I went in nonetheless and was having fun until a huge wave arose from the depths of the sea without warning.

Panicked, I scrambled to the shore toward my aunt, only to lie in that unfortunate area where the wave hits sand, where its impact and pull are the strongest. Fearing I'd be sucked into the ocean and drown, I screamed, but my aunt moved forward, grabbing my little forearms with her hands.

"I've got you," she said calmly, as the ocean continued to urge rather insistently that I join it. I felt myself slipping out of my aunt's grasp—but then, suddenly, the pull subsided, and I was safe. I could see by the wideness of my aunt's eyes that I hadn't been a baby for feeling scared.

But she'd said she had me, and she had. For the years that followed, my Aunt Trish had always had me, whether by sending me unique care packages or acting as an empathic and nonjudgmental ear.

That day at the Santa Monica Pier was fresh in my mind as I reluctantly removed myself from the freezing water, returning to the towel with my Aunt Trish. I spent the rest of the afternoon collecting interesting stones to take back to my loved ones as souvenirs—the beach was oddly littered with pebbles of every shape, texture, and color—and relaxing on the blanket, eating and drinking.

By the time we piled back into the car and headed for Santa Ynez, I felt a balance between exhaustion and peacefulness. The ocean had somehow restored something in me,

and I was happy to take relics of my visit home with me,
wherever home was.

Kindness of the Wind

I pretend the wind pushing the tree branches outside
is waves crashing against the sand of a beach—
no injury meant to the wind,
but I covet the sea
and the depth of her mysteries,
her capacity for nurturing,
free, fierce power of will,
and
destruction.
I wish
we were closer,
that we met more
than once a year.

Our meetings are magic.
She cradles me.
I hear her wisdom,
etch it into my heart,
but she washes it away

with one solid wave
replacing it with New.
Her sageness is ancient
but ever-changing
as quicksilver.
In the crest of her wave, I listen
as she threads seaweed in my hair,
wrinkles my skin.

Sometimes the wind meets us there,
drying me along with the sun
as I lie on the beach,
exhausted.
The wind listens to the ocean,
tries to remember the sound
of her waters flowing, never still,
and the wind imitates her for me
on nights at home
when I'm feeling unsure.
How sweet the wind is, how thoughtful,
but it is not the same
as the sea.

New Beginnings

EVEN AMID THE TRANQUILITY of California, my life back in Cincinnati was still on my mind. My Aunt Chris, who returned to Ohio two weeks into my visit, didn't give me frame-by-frame updates of what was going on with the house, but she had told me that all the possessions had been cleared out and no one was living in it any longer. My cats, Honey and Pickle, were with her in Colerain, and whatever stuff I hadn't designated as wanting to take with me was either sold, donated, or put into storage. In some ways, I was beyond grateful for not having to actually move things out of my home and see it slowly empty of all personality. In others, though, I felt detached and ignorant as to what was going on.

The question of schooling was also weighing on my mind. Basically, I had three options: attend an all-girls Catholic school as my aunt and grandparents preferred; attend the district school, Colerain; or apply to a new school that had only recently come to my attention: the School for Creative & Performing Arts (SCPA) in downtown Cincinnati. Though I'd never heard of it before, I was intrigued by SCPA. Given my rocky history with Catholicism and my quiet disdain for the orthodox, SCPA seemed like the optimal choice. Plus, I was eager to refine my newfound interest in writing, as well as continue with my musical education. I slowly began gathering information about SCPA, coming to learn that it was a fourth through twelfth grade school that specialized in seven areas of the arts: technical theater, drama, instrumental music, vocal music, visual arts, creative writing, and dance, as well as, of course, basic academics. The school was located in an area of Cincinnati called Over-the-Rhine, widely regarded as one of the most crime-ridden parts of town, but I didn't initially pay much attention to this fact. I was seduced by the uniqueness of the school: I could barely imagine a place where the arts, not sports, were the most valued pastime—where my habit of writing could potentially pay off. I put together a portfolio of writing samples and shipped it off to the school while I was still in California. Though I was entirely uncertain as to whether or not I would get in, I found the summer reading list on the English Department's web page and eagerly began reading and writing the papers.

My efforts, of course, didn't go unnoticed by my Aunt Trish, who took this as a sign I wouldn't be staying on with her in California. Being both a lover of diplomacy and a hater of confrontation, I never directly told her I wouldn't be staying and she never asked. Though she was probably disappointed, she supported my endeavors, which ranged from

getting my junior high to fax my transcripts, to getting Aunt
Chris to set up an interview, to me completing the prerequi-
site material for the major for which I'd be auditioning: creative writing. I scrambled to get everything together as the
final audition date for the upcoming school year drew nearer.

In the end, it was my interview at SCPA that brought me
back to Cincinnati, causing me to finally put a return date on
what had been an open-ended plane ticket. After a month's
stay in California and a great deal of resting, thinking, healing, and learning, I was ready to pursue what I envisioned to
be the best path for me at the time. With tears in my eyes, I
said good-bye to my Aunt Trish and thanked her for all she'd
done for me, feeling sorry our plans hadn't worked out the
way we'd hoped but confident I was doing what was right.

Adjustment

IN SPITE OF MY excitement for the SCPA interview,
returning to Ohio wasn't easy. On the drive home from the
airport with my grandparents and aunt, I expounded upon all
the things I'd learned and the experiences I'd had with great
zeal, unwilling to show the anxiety and sadness I was feeling
at the prospect of going to Aunt Chris's condo instead of my

house. When we pulled up to the condo complex I knew so well, my grandparents having lived there since my birth, I took a deep breath and lugged my suitcase upstairs, trying my best to be optimistic.

The room that had once been a spare bedroom and a place for my cousin Andrew to stay on occasion was now my bedroom, housing all my things. My cats had moved in and were anxious to see me. I slowly began unpacking my suitcase, trying to shake the sensation that I wasn't home yet, that this was just a layover and I shouldn't get too comfortable.

I tried not to dwell on my living situation as I prepared for my audition. On the big day, I dressed professionally in black dress pants, a white camisole, and a black blazer. I wore one of my mother's gold necklaces around my neck and carried one of my father's rings in my pocket. To me, this was more than just an attempt to get into a high school. Though I had backup plans, I didn't accept any of them. "If you don't get in here, you're going to go to McAuley," my aunt had said. I had nothing personal against McAuley High School, the all-girl alma mater of my mother and a few of my aunts, but in my heart, I didn't feel it was the right place for me.

So for me, this interview was the only option. I didn't know what I'd do if I didn't get in. Though I hadn't started writing seriously since earlier that year, I wanted SCPA with an intensity I was familiar with, and I wouldn't let myself fail.

My grandfather drove me downtown, all the necessary materials in my hands and butterflies in my stomach. Though it was simple enough to gather some writing samples and send them to a woman I didn't know—the creative writing teacher, Joy Fowler—it was quite another to sit with her face-to-face and explain why I felt I deserved to attend SCPA.

I checked in and waited for my turn to arrive. When it did, I acted with a cool professionalism that I hoped masked my true anxiety. But contrary to my notions, Dr. Joy wasn't a mean woman who was bent on ripping me apart. She was a middle-aged, soft- but clear-spoken woman with pleasant hands and long, wavy hair the color of iron. She wore gold, half-moon glasses, a long, old-fashioned dress, and socks and Birkenstocks. Her eyes were hazel, contrasting against her olive skin and sleet-colored hair: they were sharp and quick, but simultaneously warm and empathetic. So I didn't feel awkward explaining my recent change in circumstances to her after she'd given me feedback on my portfolio and asked me a few general questions.

"I'm so sorry for your loss," she said sincerely, letting her words take up the space they deserved. "But I'm very glad to have you with us."

Not letting my hopes climb too high—I wouldn't find out whether or not I was accepted until a few days later—I thanked Dr. Joy for her time and met up with my grandfather.

My good feeling turned out to be correct. I'd been accepted into SCPA, and I'd never felt happier—for the first time in a while, I felt like I had at least some control over my future. I would be pursuing a unique high school career and spending my days in a creative environment.

It was only after I was accepted that the logistics of attending SCPA settled in; namely, how I would get to school. Since my aunt worked relatively close to our home and my new school was far out of the way, being driven was not an option. Taking the city metro bus was my only choice. Though I wasn't averse to this for any snobbish reasons, the prospect did make me, a timid suburban girl, slightly nervous. The idea of passing unaccompanied through some of the most urban parts of town frightened me, much as I'm embarrassed to admit that now. Wisely, my aunt rode the bus with me to school once so I'd get a feel for the process, then had me ride it by myself a few days before school. I felt like a baby, being escorted and eased into such a simple concept, but I knew it was necessary. I was vaguely aware that it was going to be a different world, though just how different, I didn't know . . . yet.

When on the Bus

I.

There is a woman on the bus
who does not let go of her cigarette.
It rests patiently between her fingers,
unlit, whole, and full of potential,
just waiting to be inserted
between her thin, chapped lips.
She wears sweatpants and a T-shirt
and holds her cigarette
even as she kisses her child
on his yellow head,
smiling down upon him
with lips yearning for her cigarette.
As soon as they get off the bus
she lights it.
With a drag and a grin,
she is satisfied.

II.

There is a man on the bus
with two pieces of luggage.
He is quiet and stressed

and looks about the bus frequently,
features taut.
He leans on his knees into the aisle
and an older man asks him to lean back
so he can see out the window
for his stop.
The luggage man tells him
to shut the hell up.
This unbidden hostility disturbs me
and amuses others.
I later learn that he'd been seeking a flight
since morning
and had failed to make it out.
"Do I get off here?"
he asks the driver.
I wonder if he's going home.

New School, New World

MY FIRST DAY AT SCPA proved to be strange, to say the least. I woke up early, jittery and anxious, and dressed in the outfit I'd put together the day before. I rode the bus without incident, though I was paranoid the entire time, especially when a man with apparent mental deficiencies told me he liked my purse. But I survived. I even survived the two-block walk from the bus stop to school, during which I pictured myself getting hopelessly lost.

Though I made it to school, I didn't quite make it to class, instead spending most of the morning in the main theater, which had been turned into a holding ground for displaced students. Apparently something was wrong with my schedule, and the school had no printout for me to follow. I sat quietly, reading, until someone handed me a temporary schedule, which I proceeded to read incorrectly, consequently going to lunch twice and missing my biology class. In any case, I had missed what I'd most been looking forward to—creative writing. So the rest of the day passed in relative quiet as I suffered through gym, English, and world history. I rode the bus home and collapsed.

The next day was better. My schedule ironed out, I now knew I was to go to Dr. Joy's class at the sound of the first bell. Slipping in quietly without looking at anyone, I took a seat at a table where only one other girl was sitting. I busied myself with putting my bag under the table and getting paper out when the girl's words cut into my consciousness:

"You just had to ruin it, didn't you?"

I looked up, wide-eyed in confusion.

"I was sitting here alone, the table all to myself," she continued, "and you had to ruin it for me." She said it with a smile on her face, but I had no idea if she was kidding or not.

"I'm sorry," I said in a small voice.

She laughed. "Oh, it's okay, I guess," she said and began talking to someone else.

This girl, I later found out, was named Gillis, and she was just one of the many characters in my writing class. True to my wallflower mentality, rather than talking to these people, I'd sit back, watch them, and classify them: Ashley and Avery were the smart ones. They would usually sit together and answer Dr. Joy's questions when no one else would. Heather and KJ were new, like me, but both juniors; Heather was a slight blond girl who was also a visual art major, and KJ was a tall black boy with dreadlocks who wrote captivating spoken word. There was Alexa, a part Puerto Rican, part African American, part German girl with curly hair and an uncanny interest in Hitler; and Brianna, a black girl with a kind round face who had equal parts spunk and sweetness. There was Keegan, a tough-looking Irish kid who was, interestingly, one of the few people I talked to regularly, and Caprice, a soulful African American girl who was always friendly to me. There were also several other classmates who didn't speak up as much.

Dr. Joy decided to have a theme for each week. The first week's theme, at the suggestion of a girl named Megan, was self-introduction. Through our written assignments, which we shared at the end of the week, I learned fragments of information about everyone and enjoyed listening. But when the time came to read mine, I was nervous. Not sharing wasn't an option though, so I approached the podium, trying my best not to scan the crowd.

I clutched my piece in my hands. I had grappled over what to write about. *What part of me do I want these people to see first?* I'd wondered. Having not even spoken to most of them, I knew what I wrote about would be of critical importance in their first impressions of me, and even drafted a few different versions. In the end, though, I decided to read the one I'd written about my racial identity, about being "mixed," as people were apt to term it.

Without preamble, I launched in. "People call me 'mixed,' as if I were paint or some other inanimate substance to be blended and manipulated." To my relief, my opening line drew a few laughs, and by the piece's end, I was greeted with warm applause. KJ smiled at me as I took my seat, and I felt slightly more at ease regarding my place in the class.

But even if I felt I belonged there as a writer, I never thought I'd quite be one of "them." Instead of talking to the people around me, I spent idle moments writing in a notebook I shared with Abby and Kelsey back in West Chester. Whenever we saw each other, we'd switch notebooks, thus keeping up on each other's thoughts. Clinging to the notebook helped me feel connected to my old friends and not completely alone at my new school.

One day, when Dr. Joy was sick, my creative writing classmates sat together around a table, laughing and playing cards. I watched but didn't join in. And it wasn't for lack of opportunity. No one was outright mean to me, and a few people, like Heather, Keegan, KJ, Alexa, and Caprice, even made efforts to talk to me. But I just wasn't into it. Making sure I said the right thing and coming off as clever seemed like way too much work when I was still dealing with the loss of my father, moving into a new house, and attending a totally different school. Though most everyone seemed genuinely interesting and I would have liked to know them better, it was just easier for me, the wallflower, to sit off to the side. In a way, I was pleased with myself for creating what I hoped would come off as a mysterious yet intelligent persona. In other ways—in deeper ways—I was upset with myself for not actively seeking acceptance and building new friendships.

My academic classes were even worse, socially speaking. I barely talked to anyone in biology, history, or English. And then there was algebra. My teacher, I was convinced, was "a Cajun monster from hell," as I once described him in a diary entry. Mr. Samis was a loud man who seemed to feel the appropriate volume level for speaking was what most others would consider shouting. He didn't let us use calculators in class, had an extremely specific format in which we were to complete homework, and was deeply dissatisfied if we spent his class time doing anything other than algebra, as I soon found out. Shortly after I was placed in his class, I opened my book to read after completing the homework he'd assigned. Retribution was swift.

"Put it away!" came a hideous bellow from above me. I looked up in panic.

"Do some work, Ms. Shannon," he said in disgust. "*Math* work." And he stalked away.

Shaken, I did the only thing I supposed I could do as a girl who had barely been yelled at her whole life and certainly not for simply reading: I cried. I don't know if Mr. Samis or anyone else noticed. I partially hoped my teacher would, so he would apologize. But if Mr. Samis realized I was crying, he didn't say anything.

So I hated him for a while, and, as a result, doubled my efforts in his subject, eager to do my math not only correctly, but also without error in his punctilious format. Each day that he checked my work over and had no criticism to offer was a triumph. Ironically, the hard work that was intended to spite Mr. Samis led him to a sort of respect for me. I'd become one of the "good kids," the quiet ones who always did their homework. Even so, I was wary, until one day when I realized that first impressions—or impressions in general—are not always correct.

On the year's anniversary of my father's death, a local news channel had apparently shown a short tribute to him on the nightly newscast. The next day before the bell rang for algebra, Mr. Samis called me up to his desk. Supposing he was going to yell at me for something, I prepared for the worst and was thus extremely surprised when he went on to say, "I saw the news story about your father on the news last night. I'm very sorry."

I was so shocked, I could barely formulate a response. Not only had this man who had described himself as "mean, nasty, and ugly" on the first day of school seen the story about my dad, he'd cared enough to mention it to me the next day. After that, anytime someone would insult Mr. Samis or talk about how much they hated his class, I would defend him.

Lost in the Shuffle

IN SPITE OF MY NEWFOUND chumminess with my algebra teacher, I was making no strides with my peers by the second semester of school. I expounded upon the situation in a LiveJournal entry:

So, so, so, so bored.

Pretty much, my social life at SCPA . . . sucks. Time for some soul cleansing and such.

Begin emo rant.

So, I haven't really been talking to anyone. I haven't been trying to make friends. So people just think I'm weird, or emo, or quiet, or all three. Or they just talk to me because I'm smart and can help them with whatever. And I don't exactly appreciate that; but hey, it's understandable.

So yeah. While everyone's making friends and talking—new kids included—I just sit on the sidelines like a jackass. I mean, I've been shy all my life, but I still had plenty of friends. It never was a problem. But now, where I'm going into a situation where I have no one, it is a big problem.

It's like I have so much to say, but I just can't say it. Something holds me back. I'm afraid they won't listen, or they'll think I'm stupid. It's just like everyone feels bad for me even though they don't even know about my situation.

And I hate it so much. The whole thing sucks, because I like the school, and I know I'd be having a good time if I had my friends there. But they aren't, and they never will be. So it just sucks. I drag my ass down there every day, try to write, fail to speak to anyone, and come back here, only to repeat the whole thing again.

To be fair: I do appreciate the writing part of it. It's not all I'd hoped it to be, but I am growing as a writer. And that's always good.

But I miss my friends in West Chester. I miss doing things with them and going places, being with people my age and not worrying about what they'll think of me—just being Chelsey and having a great time. And sometimes I wish I were going to the freshmen building with them. It would be the typical high school experience, cliques included, but at least I wouldn't be so damn lonely.

And then, to top it all off, it's pretty much all my fault. I've barely exerted any effort.

deep breath

End emo rant.

In addition to this social maladjustment, I was continuing to deal with the culture shock of going from living in a suburban, middle class, predominantly white area to attending a school located in a very rough part of town with a great deal of cultural diversity. The diversity didn't bother me, but it did open my eyes as to how much I had missed out on when it came to half of my heritage. Around me, I heard people—white *and* black—speaking in Ebonics and using slang I was neither familiar with nor understood. Cultural references went miles over my head, and as I struggled to keep up, I underwent a minor crisis of racial identity, which had always loomed at the back of my mind as a biracial girl.

By societal standards, I acted like a white girl. I didn't listen to hip-hop or rap, or watch BET. Frankly, I didn't know what a weave was and never fully understood why my father was so adamant about me applying lotion to my elbows and knees until I started attending SCPA. But even as I learned about the part of my cultural background that had somehow been excluded from my experience, I still felt separated from other black kids, not only because of the lightness of my skin, but by my culturally homogenous background.

The Anniversary

IN MY FORMER naïve perception, cities weren't places to spend a lot of time in. They were considered dangerous in comparison to our sheltered suburbs. In spite of my father's upbringing in Cincinnati, my own exposure to the area was limited to the occasional trip to the downtown Macy's for Christmas shopping or the Museum of Natural History and Science. Walking down city streets made me nervous, even as I slowly conquered my fear of the bus.

I had never quite been aware of the relative affluence of my former home until I began attending SCPA. Occasionally, kids would make jeers about West Chester and how rich and spoiled people who lived there were. The first time I heard such a comment, I was too surprised to feel remotely offended. And when I considered it, the people of West Chester did lead fairly charmed lives. Most of my friends and neighbors had lived in large houses, as my dad and I had, complete with kitchens stocked with food and fancy appliances and family rooms hooked up with cable, a widescreen television, and the latest gaming systems. Large wardrobes and expensive handbags were the norm. Of course, I knew every family in West Chester didn't live in such comfort, nor am I suggesting that those who did were selfish or decadent. But I did come to realize that not *every-one* lived so comfortably.

Attending class with kids from a spectrum of backgrounds helped me gain perspective on my own life and place in the world. I was also exposed to kids with piercings in odd places and hair dyed odd colors, as well as many kids who were openly homosexual or bisexual, neither of which were the norm in West Chester. I embraced these aspects of SCPA, considering them positive by-products of an environment where creativity was honored. Though SCPA was far from perfect, it was supportive of kids of all different ideologies, backgrounds, colors, and personal styles. I felt myself settle into a wonderfully chromatic and vivacious student body, even if I did so quietly and without drawing much attention to myself.

It was while I was finally starting to adjust to my new life that the one-year anniversary of my father's death arrived. That day, my dad's side of the family picked me up from school to head over to the cemetery and then to a small gathering at my Aunt Carolyn's house. Since my dad's death, I'd been spending more and more time with his siblings and their children, building distinct relationships with them that I had, for some reason, missed out on while my dad was alive.

I rode quietly in the backseat as we made our way to Walnut Hills Cemetery, reflecting on a year gone by.

In some ways, everything felt so different, like my life in West Chester with Dad was eons ago, instead of just a year. Simultaneously, the pain and disbelief I still felt at his death was so fresh, it sometimes felt as though he had been killed only days earlier. I was almost shocked when I considered the adjustments I'd made to my daily life, and, even more profound, that I had endured one of the worst losses I could imagine. In the beginning, I'd thought the grief would kill me—that it would be just too much to bear. And yet, here I was. True, I was secluded and hadn't made many friends. I usually went straight home after school, crawled into bed, and watched television until it was time to go to sleep. And sometimes, when it did become too much, I'd simply weep. But somewhere within me, I knew that all my despair and pain was temporary. I knew that although this was enormously difficult, I would one day overcome it and be the happy girl I'd once been, however alien that girl seemed at the same time.

When we reached the cemetery, I joined the small semi-circle of my family members peering down at my father's grave, where I could so well remember laying him to rest. By then, there was a headstone, reading simply "Blair E.

Shannon. June 1, 1959–January 19, 2006. Son, Father, Brother, Husband." The sight was relatively new to me. I didn't come to the cemetery frequently, maintaining that it was only a body, that my father's essence was around us, within us. But it felt appropriate to pay respect to his spirit in this way.

Once everyone had arrived, I read a piece my family had asked me to prepare for the occasion.

1/19/07

Dear Daddy,

A year has gone by since you died. I reflect on the past year without you, and wonder to myself, have I become a better person? Are you proud of who I am now? Have any of us changed?

A year ago today, you were still living. You were vivacious, full of life and light. A year ago tonight, you were gone, with such caustic abruptness that took us all by the most unpleasant surprise.

You were not there to stand with us when we bore the horrible news—for once, you were not there for me to cling to or lean on. I'd endured deaths before, but you'd been there for me. This time, you were the one who was gone. My pillar of strength had been demolished, and I was totally lost.

The next few months were a blur for me, as I'm sure they were for many of us. I felt like I was in a daze, some sort of prolonged, demented nightmare that would not let up, no matter how much I wished it away. I simply could not believe that my dad, Blair Shannon, was dead—killed, no less. Though you were human and mortal, it somehow seemed illogical in my mind that you could really be gone.

Moving out of the house was really hard for me. I knew it had to be done, but you and I had many memories there. Whenever we go back to get something from there now, I am filled with pain and reminded of you. There is no home for me without you.

I think everybody has been having a hard time, even people who don't say much about it. It's hard for me, because you were always there for me to talk to, and now you're gone. I guess people think I'm doing okay. I'm not a lot of the time—the year has been extremely trying for me, as could be expected—but I will be okay, eventually. I'm not rushing anything.

A lot of people—Americans, especially—seem to think that once a year of grieving has passed, the worst part is over, and we should all move on. It's not like that at all. Anyone who's ever lost someone they loved knows there is no formula or set amount of time that will ease the pain. I feel I haven't even started yet; I've been too preoccupied with moving and start-

ing at a different high school.

What hurts the most is that you were killed, and no one has been caught so far. I hope everyday that something will be done—that some sort of justice will be served. It would certainly make me feel better, but I know that wouldn't bring you back. That wouldn't erase the pain we've all felt over this past year. Although I honestly hope your killer will be caught, I doubt he ever will be. But if any kind of karma exists, I'm certain he'll get what's coming to him.

Your being gone now makes me appreciate all the special little things you did for me. Like the way you packed my lunches, or the notes you'd leave me in the morning, or how you'd call me every day you could while you were gone. Since you were such a good dad to me, I feel very deprived now, but I would rather have had a great dad for a short time than a bad dad for my whole life any day.

I hope you're proud of me, going to a totally different school and all. I think you'd be surprised at some of the things I do every day. I've been trying to be brave for you and try new things.

I think everyone should take some time today to think of how things have changed: who they've grown closer to, who they've drifted apart from, how perceptions of our own selves have changed, what is important to us now, and, of course, *special memories of you.*

I think of you every day, and I'm pretty sure most of the people here today do as well. I don't know what happens in the afterlife, but I hope very much that I will see you again. Even though I can't hug you anymore or hear you tell me you love me, I carry you in my heart every day. You're a part of me always.

Love,

Chelsey Kimberly Shannon, Your Peanut

My family thanked me for my words, and after a few prayers were said and tears were shed, we ate a light dinner at my Aunt Carolyn's and watched a copy of the slideshow that had played at my dad's funeral. In some ways, since the pain and absence were no longer a shock, I was able to feel their effects more fully. This time, I cried with abandon.

In spite of my sadness over the circumstances, I felt happy that I felt comfortable enough with my dad's side of the family to share such an occasion with them. I hadn't grown up feeling especially close to my father's brothers, Myron and Lester, or his sister, Carolyn, but we seemed to have bonded during our family tragedy, as is bound to happen. I found myself beginning to spend time with my uncles and aunt outside of family holiday gatherings, as well as my dad's niece—my cousin Shaunda—and her family. I was grateful to finally build relationships with people who had known my dad with a similar intimacy as I had.

Still Adjusting

SINCE I'D MOVED INTO my aunt's condo months earlier, I was finally beginning to feel more comfortable. I'd painted my room (albeit a pale green that I later regretted) and rearranged the furniture to my liking. Things with my Aunt Chris were still rocky, however. It wasn't so much that our relationship was flawed. The more I dwelled on it, the more I realized that there was one main source of our problems: my Aunt Chris was not my dad. This was, obviously, neither of our faults. The move was a big adjustment for us both. Having already raised her own kids, my aunt probably never imagined she'd have to take on another teenager. Even if only in my own mind, I felt the need to walk on eggshells, to never mess up.

You're not hers, I reasoned. *She's under no obligation to keep you here.* And, sometimes, if I was feeling particularly sad, I'd think, *She doesn't really want you here.*

Going from my laid-back, permissive dad, to my

structured, type A Aunt Chris was also a major shift. While my dad had no qualms about spending lazy days at home doing nothing but watching movies, my aunt saw free days as perfect opportunities to clean the house, or, if the house was already clean, to "get organized," one of her favorite euphemistic phrases. We also experienced the basic clashes that naturally arise when you share a living space with a new person.

The worst memory I have of my early days of living with my aunt was during a time that occurred in late autumn. I had just been visiting a bookstore and called my aunt to ask her to pick me up on her way home from work. In retrospect, I fully acknowledge my tone was rather bossy and impolite. But at the time, I had no such notion and thus was surprised when, after being picked up and heading down to my grand-parents' condo to say hello, I walked in the room to hear my aunt complaining to them about my behavior.

"I am not her maid," she said fiercely.

It was one of those awkward situations where you walk in at just the wrong moment. Objectively, I knew what she said was true. She *wasn't* my maid, and I should have asked her for a ride more nicely. But in my fragile emotional state, any expression of discontent concerning me—especially one not addressed to me directly—was only indicative of the fact that

I was a nuisance, that Aunt Chris didn't really want me around. I began to cry in spite of myself as I made my presence known. My grandma rose to comfort me.

"I just asked for a ride," I said through my tears. "Jesus Christ," I added before I could stop myself. Big mistake. Any derivative of God's name used in vain should never be uttered in the presence of strident Catholics or there would be hell to pay. Their response was swift and full of outrage. My aunt rose from her chair to chastise me, both she and my grandma barraging me: "You must *never* say that."

This reaction upset me further. They seemed far more shaken by my use of language than how upset I was. I dashed into my grandma's bathroom and locked the door, settling onto the floor, light still off. My grandma came and knocked softly on the door after a few moments, but I didn't respond. After a while my family left me alone, and my tears intensified, becoming shuttering sobs that escalated into hyperventilation at intervals. I attempted to calm myself down, but whenever I thought of my aunt's words or my grandmother's disappointment, it became harder and harder to breathe.

The bigger picture hurt too. *I don't belong here*, I thought miserably. *What the fuck am I doing here? I'll never be happy. I might as well die.*

A half hour went by in this manner, me lying on the floor,

attempting not to pass out from hyperventilation. Partially, I didn't leave for so long because I was truly upset; partially, I didn't leave because I didn't want to face my aunt, who was apparently so dissatisfied with me.

As I splashed cool water on my face after finally calming down, I heard someone come into the adjacent bedroom. Preparing myself for a continuation of the conflict, I was surprised to find my grandpa standing there when I opened the door. He opened his arms to me, and I laid my head on his shoulder, beginning to cry again. He gently rubbed my back and didn't ask for an apology or say anything, understanding that sometimes words are simply unnecessary. He led me back into the kitchen, where my aunt and grandma were sitting at the table. I slunk down into my seat, unable to look either of them in the eye. Though I wasn't ashamed of my language, I did regret upsetting them, and I knew they likely didn't understand why I was so upset, probably finding my reaction babyish and histrionic. I didn't feel like explaining I wasn't just upset because Aunt Chris was annoyed with me. It would have raised too many questions—and drawn too many words of placation—to explain that I was upset because I felt like a bother.

Instead, I apologized to my aunt for acting like a brat and using God's name in vain. She apologized for upsetting me.

I ate a bowl of cottage cheese, and my aunt and grandma joked lightly for the rest of the meal. Soon, the incident was forgotten, but I couldn't let go of all the huge feelings Aunt Chris's simple words had brought up for me—that at the end of the day, I was an imposition.

My daily life living with Aunt Chris took some getting used to. My life with my dad had been unique, especially because he was gone for roughly two weeks out of the month. But when he was home, he was very much *home*. He ran errands during the day, leaving afternoons and evenings free to be spent with me. This was probably how we developed such a strong relationship in spite of his absences. When we were at home together, we would spend a lot of time talking, watching movies, and eating leisurely meals. We were aware of each other's quirks, likes, and annoyances, and were comfortable in each other's company.

With my Aunt Chris, there wasn't as much free time. She worked regular hours as a nurse, and after getting off, she was often required to spend an hour or two at the barn to take care of her horses. By the time she came home, exhausted, she didn't feel much like talking, and frankly, after a long day of school, riding the bus, chores, and homework, neither did I. So rather than spending evenings together as my dad and I probably would have, my aunt passed the hours before bed in the family room while I sequestered myself in my room. I just didn't have the energy to try to build a relationship like the one I'd had with my dad, especially when I'd been forced to realize even the strongest relationships can end suddenly and traumatically.

The sad part of it was, before I'd moved in with her, my aunt and I had enjoyed each other's company as aunt and niece. We would do fun things together and not worry about rules or stepping on eggshells. Though we were (and are) very different people, we'd try to do things the other person liked, compromising and trying out new activities. My aunt even expressed her sadness at losing this fun, lighter aspect of our relationship following her assumption of guardianship over me. Maybe she felt the only way for her to be my guardian was through an outlined set of rules and a stern stance. In some ways, she was right. My childhood hadn't had much structure, having been shaken up by the death of my mother and my dad's unusual career. Though I enjoyed the lack of ordinariness, part of me had always craved structure. I would make chore charts, budgets, and to-do lists for fun. I made an hour-by-hour schedule of how to spend my summer days and stuck to it. Now, instead of me being responsible for adding organization to my life, someone else was doing it for me. Though I enjoyed structure to an extent, this didn't always mean I enjoyed the idea of someone else imposing it on me. I would sometimes fight with my aunt over stupid things like doing the dishes, or give her attitude when she asked me to clean my room. Even in my own ears, I sounded like a brat. But I didn't care.

These setbacks were comparatively minor, however. What most bothered me about my relationship with my aunt was how lukewarm it was—how the condo still didn't feel like home to me after six months of living there. I wondered if it ever would.

Home

You could say the house was sacred,
and i dream of it often,
floors tread upon all my years,
grooves and creaks old friends,
walls painted beige then fuchsia then pumpkin,
and i was there for it all.
The red leather sectional was my refuge,
the little-used green-pink living room
the temple of my thoughts,
my energy scattered and shared,
encased by the red brick exterior.
I thought it was the place that made the peace,
the safe,

the warmth—
or at least,
i thought it had some power of its own.
But when you left,
home died.
When you left,
home became a house.
Now, in my dreams,
it doesn't even feel like home
when you're there too.

Remembering

AS I CONTINUED TO settle into SCPA and the condo in Colerain, I was still very much adjusting to the reality that my father was gone. I was also becoming deeply aware of the effect of having lost in my life a loved one who was murdered as opposed to dying of illness or old age. With my father's death, there was more anger—though not necessarily at the person who had actually killed him. I was angry at the situation more than anything. That my father had been taken away by a person, not a disease or time, made his death seem all the more unfair. Though I tried not to think of it much, the idea of Dad dying in such agony and fear pained me on a fundamental level. It wasn't the same with my mother, who had slowly winded down, and who had likely known she was dying, however terrible that was in its own right. With my dad, minutes before he died, he'd been bright and vivacious as ever—then suddenly, he was simply gone.

My Aunt Erin in California initiated a lawsuit for negligence against the hotel my dad and Monique had stayed in that night. As Monique had described it, the entire establishment had been shady, and though they had balconies that were accessible from the street, they hadn't had any security cameras.

Though I didn't think a lawsuit would hurt matters, I didn't devote myself to the idea, nor to the idea of my dad's murderer being caught. The way I saw it, he was a faceless, nameless criminal, and for all we knew, he could be dead now, or moved away, or have changed his mind about the way his life was going. Maybe he had never committed a crime before. Or maybe he had a long history of such incidents. We'd never know. I tried not to concern myself with the details and legal aspects of my dad's death. Though such a familiar, pragmatic approach probably comforted some of my family members—the most natural thing to do when someone you love is harmed is to seek justice—I preferred to deal with the emotional side of things.

At the same time, however, I couldn't imagine what Monique must have been going through each day, having seen my father die and having been in the room in his last moments. I couldn't imagine the blame she must have laid on herself, the tortured wonderings of *What if*, always *What if*. Though we hadn't been very close during my father's lifetime, Monique and I began spending more time together following his death, partially because, in some ways, she was the closest person I had to my dad, since they were together during so many of his final days on earth, and partially because I knew I was the closest person *she* had to my dad.

One day, while driving home from an outing together, we started talking about my father as we often did. Monique began to describe my dad's final day with an attention to detail I'd never heard before. Her voice broke when she began to describe my dad jumping up from the bed when he heard someone slide the balcony door open, and she paused.

"I'm sorry," she said. "You probably don't want to hear this."

"No," I replied gently, but honestly, "I do." I had an almost morbid curiosity about that short window of time when my father had gone from living to dead.

She described to me how they'd passed the day and evening, how they'd been sleeping peacefully when my dad awoke to the sound of the balcony door opening, how alertly and quickly he sprang from the bed. She told me how she panicked, how she wouldn't be quiet, no matter how many times the intruder—a young man holding a gun—shushed her. She said he was agitated, standing in the balcony bathed in light, maybe because he was afraid someone would see his failed attempted robbery. She said my dad was calm, that even in such a moment of fear and chaos, he was sure and still as the earth, attempting to reason with the man, saying he could have anything he wanted as long as he harmed no one. But the man was too agitated and shot into the room before running off, gaining nothing, taking so much.

Monique told me how my dad sat calmly on the hotel bed and picked up the phone to call the front desk. "Call an ambulance; I've been shot." But it was too late. The bullet had hit him in the chest, the precious receptacle of human life. He sunk quietly to the ground with a grace, Monique said, you wouldn't expect of a man his size, but what more could you expect from my father—charming, genteel Blair? It was only fitting that he died quietly, with a dignity and serenity that I never could have mustered if I was laying on the floor, knowing my life was quietly draining out of me. Monique knelt beside him as his breathing stilled, comforting him as best she could. How could you comfort a dying man who had so much life and so much to live for? What could you do or say?

She told me how slowly the paramedics moved when they arrived, as if they knew it was already too late. She said they were inattentive and almost casual, an attitude that infuriated her. And then he was taken away in the ambulance to a hospital where he was pronounced dead.

There are things about her story I'll never understand. Why my father? Why my family? Why did the bullet have to hit his chest? Why couldn't the ambulance have been faster? Why hadn't they stayed in another hotel? And, more deeply, what did my father think of in those last, fading moments? Did he cling to the hope that this would be righted, that it would turn into a frightening but ultimately safe travel anecdote to tell to friends? Did he think he would see my face again, or did he blame himself for leaving me an orphan? Or were his last moments tranquil as his demeanor, quietly accepting, if gently regretful?

I'll never know. None of us will. But as Monique finished telling me the story, breaking into soft tears, I felt her pain, the pain of my father, and, acutely, my own loss. I sincerely hoped my dad's final thoughts hadn't been ones of anger or remorse or blame, but ones of acceptance, peace, and love for those he was leaving behind. Given the type of person he was, they probably were.

Awake

Back from my break,
I'm here,
ready to live again,
ready to feel my lungs
expand with air
again.
My hibernation—
self-induced isolation—
is gone now
(I hope forever),
and I am ready to live.
I am ready to be.
So I spread out my fragile wings
and fly.

Reevaluation

WITH THE SPRING, something began to change within me. As the earth slowly awakened, bursting into bloom, I began to disentangle myself from the web of sorrow and isolation that had ensnared me since my dad's death. I'm not sure why, exactly, because sadness and solitude were comfortable for me, if not enjoyable. Maybe it was because it had been over a year since my dad had died, and I knew he wouldn't want me to be so sorrowful on his account. Maybe it was because I refused to continue to feel dead inside as the world around me sprang into life, enjoying its youth. Renowned developmental psychologist Erik Erickson's theory of psychosocial development states that adolescence is a period devoted to developing one's identity. If anything, mine had been lost amid the grief, turmoil, and stress of moving to a new school. Though I had spent a lot of time with myself in reflection and healing, I still felt like I didn't really know who I was. What were my values? What did I believe in? What did I like? What did I want to do with my life? All previous conceptions of these notions were thrown to the wayside with the jarring death of my dad, and I felt the need to rebuild myself from the ground up.

I consciously decided to start with religion. Uncomfortable with the idea of not really having a name for what I believed in, I decided to research different religions. I quickly learned I was no longer a Catholic, and, even further, that I no longer believed in the divinity of Jesus Christ. This was a startling realization for me, in spite of the fact that this knowledge had long been lurking in my subconscious. It's easy when rejecting one's predetermined brand of Christianity to say, "Well, I still believe in Jesus." I had said the same thing for a while to reassure my aunts and other relatives. But it simply wasn't true for me anymore. The idea of a human being so divine—divinity itself—had long been foreign to me, and suddenly I was able to say with reasonably strong conviction that I didn't believe it.

This was thrilling. I no longer felt like a pseudo-Catholic, trying and failing to adhere to a doctrine that had never resonated with me. Almost immediately, I felt truer and more at peace with myself. I began to explore non-Christian religions specifically, because I still wanted to feel I was a part of some larger group, not wanting to be thrown off as some spiritual rogue. My interest in nature and the sacredness of the earth led me to the path of Neopaganism. The concept of a nurturing, natural divinity, characterized as female, appealed to me, as did the ability to connect with the divine without the necessity of "official" intercession and the absence of absolute punishment or reward or a hierarchy of holiness. Despite my happiness with my newfound faith, I knew my aunt likely wouldn't be so pleased, even though I'd found an underlying connection between Catholicism and Paganism. Still, I felt the need to tell her about my discovery. I wanted to be open and honest about who I was becoming.

It took awhile for me to gather the courage to speak up on the topic. I decided to do so when Roger was around, so it wouldn't turn into too intense of a conversation, or, even worse, an ugly one. One evening, as we dined at Red Lobster, I sat up straight, looked them both in the eyes, and said I had something to tell them.

"I don't believe in Jesus," I said simply.

Their reaction wasn't as extreme as I'd feared, but it wasn't warm, either.

"Why not?" my aunt asked. I didn't really have an answer. To me, the real question was, why would I? Why did she believe in Jesus, or God, or Heaven? Faith isn't something anyone is born with. It has to be cultivated. The default, if you think about it, is to *not* believe. It's not as if we're born with an innate sense of loyalty to a certain religion or any religion at all. It's something that is learned and practiced as one grows older, if one chooses to do so. And, after much conscious thought, I realized a traditionally religious path wasn't right for me.

My aunt, on the other hand, was the opposite. Religion was one of the most valued aspects of her life. She always strove to be a good Catholic and cherished the notion of salvation and Heaven when times were rough. And I admired her tenacity and devotion. I had once been the same way, I had to admit. But now, from an objective standpoint, I knew I didn't need unproven, albeit pleasant, assertions to comfort myself about my parents' deaths. Though it would be lovely to believe they were sharing a cloud in Heaven watching over me, this wasn't necessarily the case, and I didn't have to comfort myself with something that may or may not be true. It was enough to me that my parents had loved me while they were alive. Though I did assert that some part of them—spirit, essence, *something*—was still around me, I didn't believe I would someday join them in Heaven or see them again.

Rather than delve into the psychology and philosophy of my decision—things I wasn't entirely clear about myself yet—I told my aunt that I no longer believed, but that I respected her spiritual beliefs and hoped she would do likewise for me. The conversation veered after that, for which I was grateful, but I knew the matter wouldn't be permanently dropped. A few times, following a morning spent in church or on the car ride home from some function or another, my aunt would bring up the topic, again asking why I didn't believe or saying she thought my change of mind was a phase. I wanted to explain my thoughts to her. I wanted her to understand I hadn't stopped believing in Christ because I had lost both of my parents early, or that my lack of faith wasn't the product of some foolish spiritual rebellion but the result of an analytical questioning of my own values and beliefs. But I never went into these explanations with my aunt, fearing they would only lead to conflict. I kept my responses concise and sparing, and she would usually move on. Even though I wanted Aunt Chris to understand me, I knew it would be hard for her to see things my way after she'd spent her whole life believing in Christ and practicing Catholicism. And even if we disagreed, I wanted our relationship to be as peaceful as possible.

New Visions

ANOTHER PART OF my newly structured identity was my vegetarianism. It was a concept that had always been a part of my peripheral consciousness: I had often given up meat for Lent as a younger child and was always compassionate toward the plight of animals. In the spring of my freshman year, I met a boy named Robert who rode the same bus home as me and was a vegetarian. Partly wanting to impress him and partly genuinely curious, I went about the task of researching vegetarianism and people's motivations in adhering to such a lifestyle. Without much effort, I was exposed to a plethora of information about the animal agriculture industry, the cruelty farm animals endure, and the health benefits of a plant-based diet. After my research, the decision to become a vegetarian was snap and without hesitation.

With my shift to vegetarianism, I became more aware of my body, its needs, and nutrition. As most vegetarians do when they make the switch, I researched what nutrients were necessary—for any human, not just plant-eaters—and how to obtain them without eating meat. Becoming a vegetarian forced me to eat more mindfully. Suddenly, I couldn't eat whatever my grandmother cooked or my aunt brought home. So, I began to prepare my own meals, mostly out of necessity. I didn't know at the time that it was the beginning of a love for cooking.

My heightened attention to my body was generally unprecedented and led to a much greater comfort in my own skin. I felt synchronized with my person. For once, my body wasn't just a shell. It was a corporeal extension of me that I was in touch with and, yes, was even beginning to like.

It wasn't perfect, of course. I still maintained excess fat on my stomach, left over from my father's period of depression after my mother's death, during which I mostly ate Chef Boyardee, as Dad wasn't feeling up to cooking. And I still maintained typical adolescent insecurities. But for the first time, I didn't feel the need to hide my body when crossing in front of a room full of people. When someone would compliment me, I would actually believe them. I took better care of myself because I actually liked my appearance. I began to see my dark, curly hair as an asset instead of an uncontrollable liability. I learned to care for my specific hair instead of following general beauty regiments. I began to drink less milk, and my sinuses cleared. I felt I had more energy. A picky child, cutting out meat forced me to try new things, namely vegetables and beans. I grew to like most of them—actually, came to like most any food when adequately prepared.

Though I was devoted to my cause, I wasn't without temptation. One memory in particular comes to mind: my cousin's graduation party. The fried chicken smelled wonderful, and there I stood, not far from it, with my mostly-empty and certainly insubstantial plate of raw vegetables and pasta salad. It would have been so easy to simply grab a piece of chicken from the steaming platter and partake, but, reflecting on the information I'd gathered about animal suffering, I knew I had no choice but to refrain. The act—and my adoption of vegetarianism in general—helped me cultivate a compassion and awareness for other beings that I had been without before, as well as the discipline to refrain from always indulging myself whenever I wanted something.

Community

IN THE EARLY SUMMER, I became involved in a wonderful organization called Women Writing for (a) Change (WWf(a)C). Imagine a quiet, calm, open room and a circle formed of large, comfortable pillows. There is a candle in the middle of the circle and girls perched on the pillows. The facilitator reads a poem to begin the class, then a stone is passed from hand to hand as each girl checks in with the group, summarizing her week up to this point and giving feedback to the poem. Then we write, responding to the poem or another prompt or whatever else comes to our minds, and we share. But absent from our sharing is any self-consciousness, or pretentiousness, or competition. We share from our hearts, and our words are received with open minds. There is no applause when a reader finishes—only a quiet, calm chime, an equal response to pieces short or long, happy or sad, lyrical or straightforward. Around you, even if the girls are strangers, you feel surrounded by love and caring.

Women Writing first entered my consciousness when I was still living in West Chester. An old friend of my father's had attended classes there and thought it would interest me when she learned I had a renewed interest in writing. However, at the time, we lived so far from the writing hall (far, interestingly enough, from everything that would play an important role in my later life) that I never pursued it. However, during freshman year, Avery, a girl from my writing class at school, would often talk about Women Writing and how much she enjoyed it. Reminded of the organization, I decided to sign up for the summer class and see what it was all about.

At first, I was self-conscious as usual, worrying my words would be judged, judging them myself. It felt strange to read something directly after I'd written it. I knew—or thought I knew—that for a piece to be exemplary, it would have to go through much editing and revision. However, within a few days of the summer class, I settled right in, comforted by the flickering of the candle, the quiet of the space, the lack of judgment from my listeners, the honest, clear voices of others.

One of my favorite aspects of Women Writing was small groups, which were exactly what they sound like. For fifty minutes, we would break from the large group into smaller, preassigned groups, in which each member received an equal amount of time to share whatever she wanted and receive whatever specific feedback she requested. I enjoyed both listening intently to others and having a concentrated period of time for my voice to be heard.

Initially, the idea of reading my work for seven or eight

uninterrupted minutes felt daunting, but once I let my defenses down and stopped worrying about criticism and skill level, I found it surprisingly easy and deeply enjoyable. Small groups also helped me learn the value of specific feedback. Like most writers, I'm familiar with having someone read a piece of my work, only to have them smile, return it, and say simply, "It's good,"—not for lack of sincerity, but for lack of knowledge of what else to say. In small groups, I was encouraged to ask for the specific feedback I wanted from my group members—whether it be questions of craft, how well I conveyed my emotions within the piece, or the emotional reaction of my listeners to the piece. If we wanted, we could even request silence. At first, when my group asked me what kind of feedback I wanted, I was tempted to respond, "I don't really care. Tell me whatever you want," not wanting to feel demanding or fussy. But the truth was, I *did* care what they told me, so I consciously made an effort to ask for specific feedback. Like many aspects of Women Writing, this is a principle I've learned to apply to life in general: ask for what you need.

Another lovely aspect of Women Writing was the read-back lines. At the end of each class, there was a read-around, which is where we went around the circle, and each person chose to read from her own work or pass to the next person. The rest of the group listened and wrote down lines or phrases from the readers' pieces that caught their ear. When everyone had read or passed, each person read the lines she had jotted down—read-back lines—in random order, sometimes slightly overlapping each other. It was a reprise of the read-around, a symphony of words. I would feel honored whenever I heard a line from my piece read back, serendipitous and united when someone else read a line I too had written down. I'd make an effort to say a read-back line at least once, to have my voice heard.

Undoubtedly, Women Writing for (a) Change helped me find my voice and, moreover, find the courage to project it without fear. Women Writing's tolerant, warm environment was the perfect place for self-discovery. I could write about virtually anything I wanted. No topic was too sad or seemingly insignificant for exploration, and my words were always met with genuine praise. Whereas I usually felt like I was wasting people's time when I shared in creative writing class at school, I felt worthy and respected at Women Writing, largely because I had learned to respect my own worth. I felt camaraderie with my fellow writers and nurtured by the facilitators. By the time the final, public read-around arrived, I felt a similar grace and ease in reading my piece as I'd felt when I read at my dad's funeral.

Aside from helping me find my voice, write from my

heart, and, eventually, come to love myself, Women Writing also introduced me to the idea of feminism. Though it had always been on the peripherals of my consciousness, I didn't really know much about it and certainly not what it meant to me. Although I realized that many people rejected the term *feminist* as extremist, I came to accept the label with open arms. Feminism, I learned, wasn't a matter of putting down men or about female supremacy—conversely, it was about gender equality, finding worth in both genders, and realizing that each person has both masculinity and femininity within them. It was quite simple and logical to me, and as soon as I thought about it I knew I was, in fact, a feminist.

West Again

SHORTLY AFTER WOMEN Writing ended, I headed out to California. My Aunt Trish was no longer tending to the house in the gated community; she and Michael were now renting a house in the same town. My time with Aunt Trish was no less valuable or connected; we continued to have long, in-depth talks, cook together, and watch films. We also made jam and took trips into Santa Barbara.

That summer, we visited another secluded beach, this one

in Santa Barbara. It took about a half-hour to walk from the parking lot down a treacherous cliff to the beach. Few bathers dotted the sand, some taking advantage of the clothing-optional policy. My aunt and I set up a towel in a secluded area of the beach. I stripped off my swimsuit and plunged into the water, the vulnerability I felt complimenting my experience that year. I'd been stripped to the core emotionally, pushed far out of my comfort zone by attending a new school, living in a new home, uncovering new parts of myself. But, along with the vulnerability, like swimming in the ocean without the protective layer of a swimsuit, there was also freedom. In my new, unbound life, I had been free to discover who I was, free to uncover any hidden potentials, build new expectations for myself. I swam a long time in the water that day, peaceful and calm, simply enjoying the sensation of being enveloped by the sea.

On that trip, I began to wonder once more if I should stay in California. Though SCPA had provided eye-opening changes, I wasn't entirely happy there. I hadn't made many friends and wondered if a girl of suburban heritage such as myself could ever fully adapt to a more urban lifestyle. Additionally, my life with my Aunt Chris was still rocky, even if it had calmed down somewhat. Simply put, I was safe, but I wasn't very happy.

As I began to talk options over with my aunts, gathering perspective and thoughts, I started wondering if I could really be happy anywhere. Of course, I was still grieving. Wasn't discontent to be expected? Wasn't it better, as I'd initially thought, to be living in a place that was at least somewhat familiar and near my old friends? At the same time, the appeal of moving to California was alluring: I could start fresh, try to forget what had happened, enjoy life in a two-parent household, and form stronger bonds with my other relatives in California. Both options—staying or going—had their merits as well as their drawbacks, and it was very difficult to decide which would be best.

By the time I left California, I felt ninety percent certain I would be returning before the end of the summer, moving in with my Aunt Trish and enrolling in the local high school. I felt excited but still slightly torn. I didn't want my Aunt Chris to think I was ungrateful for her generosity, nor did I want to upset my grandparents. The night I returned to Ohio, I decided to talk with my Aunt Chris about my pending decision.

She was already in bed when I went to her, but she agreed to talk to me anyway.

"I'm thinking about moving to California," I said bluntly.

"I know."

"What do you think about that?"

"Well," she said objectively, "I know you and Trisha have a strong bond. I think she and Michael are good for you in ways I'm not. I feel like sometimes you're looking for nurturing from me, and I'm just not really good for that."

I nodded. That was all true.

"But I want you to realize that sometimes, when you visit a place, it seems nicer than it really would be if you were there all the time."

"Yeah," I agreed. The thought had occurred to me.

"And if you move out there, you're there for the rest of high school. There won't be any back and forth." It wasn't a decision to be taken lightly.

She expressed her understanding for my desire to move, but gave me another perspective to consider. "It's been good for you to be here, so you can see your friends and Grandma and Grandpa, I think," she continued. "So maybe you should stay here for a few months, go back to school, and see if it's any better. If it's not, maybe then think about going. You can't leave right away, anyway. If you move, you have to tie things up first."

I was quiet a minute, absorbing her logic and impartial analysis. "That sounds like a good idea," I said, referring to her plan of staying in Cincinnati for a few months. It seemed like a good compromise.

"And . . . " I hesitated. "I just want you to know that I appreciate you letting me stay with you." To my surprise, I started crying. "And you've just always—" I broke off in tears, unable to finish.

"Always been there?" she asked, and I nodded. "I always will be," she continued in her matter-of-fact manner. "Whether you decide to stay here or not."

A Family of Friends

I ENDED UP DECIDING to stay in Cincinnati. After going back to SCPA and realizing what a great opportunity and unique high school experience it was, it seemed like the right choice. Though I probably would have benefited from living with my Aunt Trish and Michael, I also realized moving away wouldn't solve all my problems or allow me to forget. I couldn't just escape the situation by changing where I was living. Instead, I stayed in Cincinnati, in some ways to finish what I had started.

In the end, this turned out to be a good choice for me. The more time elapsed since moving out of my old house, the more outgoing I became, slowly growing more comfortable with revealing the newfound parts of myself to others. I made more friends at school and no longer felt I was stuck in a depressive rut.

That year, instead of being with Dr. Joy for creative writing, I was taking playwriting with Ms. Lenning, a class comprised of the other sophomore writing majors, as well as KJ, Heather, and a few new additions. Alex was new to the school, a year older than me, and a can-do fashionista who added great sparkle to our class. Kelsie was a junior who had attended SCPA the year before I had started. A fierce, loving girl, we wrote our first play together and ultimately became good friends. Sandrina was a rebel with a heart of gold. I came to think of her as a punk with endearingly obscure tastes and a sweet heart. There was also Keloni, a senior who also majored in art and was amazingly talented, but always humble. I became close to these people, as well as the others who had been in my writing class the previous year. By the end of the year, I had established a deep, meaningful connection with almost everyone in my writing class. We formed a pseudo-family of sorts, sharing phrases and inside jokes. Suddenly, I was in the midst of a wonderful community of people, each one different and adding his or her own personal flare to the group. It amazed me that I was so close to everyone when the previous year I had felt sure I would never be a part of things.

I became particularly close with Avery, a girl I had met freshman year who shared most of my non-writing classes, and who was also in my Women Writing for (a) Change class in the fall. Though I was still close with my friends from West Chester, I needed a close friend who went to the same school as me. As she was a familiar face, I began opening up to Avery in the beginning of sophomore year, exploring my newfound, if embryonic, outgoing nature. I was slightly intimidated at first, as Avery was very intelligent and an excellent writer. But the more I talked to her, the more I saw she was also a funny, interesting person and we had a lot in common.

Our friendship was cemented about a month after school began. I had been planning a dinner party for my friends from West Chester, and Avery and I were talking about food and cooking in chemistry one day.

On an excited whim, I turned to her and said, "Hey, I'm having a dinner party on Saturday. Do you want to come?"

She seemed surprised but pleased at my spontaneous invitation. "Sure," she said, nodding.

It was a curious intersection of what I'd come to think of as my old life, West Chester, and my new life, SCPA. Despite my slight anxiety, the party went well. Abby and Bridget got along well with Avery, who was brave in the face of meeting new people. We enjoyed dinner together and played Scrabble before everyone headed home. Afterwards, Abby expressed her relief and happiness that I'd found a good friend at my new school.

From there, my friendship with Avery blossomed. We enjoyed the typical movie nights and sleepovers, as well as our more unusual brand of bonding: cooking. Our conversations about food turned into ideas about what to make. Early on, impressed by my cooking at the dinner party, Avery suggested I come over to her house to bake an apple pie one day. Though we actually never made the pie, it was a charming notion to me, and I knew then that Avery and I would be close. Over the months that followed, we made chocolate French toast sandwiches, black bean burgers, spaghetti, strawberry shortcakes, fried potatoes, homemade pasta, lasagna, artichokes, cheesecake, blackberry scones, pancakes, macaroni and cheese, lemonade, and all manner of other things—all the while talking, laughing, and learning to work together.

Another signal that Avery was in my life to stay was the fact that she shared her birthday, June 1, with my dad. Unlike many people, Avery was neither uncomfortable nor overly sympathetic when I talked about my parents. In contrast to most of my friends, Avery had never met my dad, and she was always eager to hear about him.

Our friendship was further solidified by our participation in the Young Women's Feminist Leadership Academy (YWFLA), through Women Writing for (a) Change. YWFLA was a program designed to help young women cultivate general conscious leadership skills, as well as lead a writing group in the Women Writing for (a) Change style. Though I had only been participating in Women Writing for about six months, I knew it was an important place for me to be, and I was eager to participate in it in any way possible.

I never considered myself much of a leader, probably due to my lack of self-confidence. I also felt that way because I wasn't particularly bossy or assertive, qualities I thought were essential to good leadership. Through YWFLA, I learned I was wrong. YWFLA helped me gain confidence in my leadership abilities and myself in general. The program consisted of two retreats at a convent tucked away in Kentucky, as well as eight weeks of Sunday evening classes. Over this time, we learned about leadership, feminism, the sacredness of honoring our voices through writing, and how to lead consciously, not pedagogically. I became close to the other girls in my class—Jaime, Janela, Julia, Megan, Karen, Alicia, and Avery—as well as our facilitators, Jenn and Sami. I slowly became aware that there are many brands of leadership, and that the bossy, in-your-face kind isn't necessarily the best. As the time drew nearer to complete our practicum—a required project where we were to put the information and skills we had learned to practical use—I felt confident I would be able to lead a circle.

My practicum took the form of a weekly circle for seventh and eighth grade girls once a week after school. The circle lasted for seven weeks and was built around topics that had been important to me at the girls' age, like family, friends, and identity. Though I only had three girls in my group, along with the occasional attendance of my YWFLA mentor, Marissa, I felt important ideas were exchanged, and the girls seemed to find the circle a positive space for them to write and explore their thoughts and feelings. I was happy to give them a peace similar to what I'd found at Women Writing the previous summer. By the time our circle was over, I felt comfortable in my leadership abilities, and my self-confidence had grown.

At one of the YWFLA retreats, I wrote the following piece:

> After a childhood incident of attempting to light an Advent candle and getting burned in the process, I have been afraid of fire, lighting matches, and the potential for destruction that it has.

Now that I have successfully lit my first match, I feel amazingly powerful. It was frightening at first, when the match finally took and ignited, but I didn't panic, only calmly lit the candle—my candle—and quietly basked in the glory of the light. I imagined doing the same in my own circle of girls: lighting the candle that would brighten the space where their voices were to be heard. They would stare into the flame I had provided and feel safe, worthy, held.

Humbled yet amazed, I realized I had the power to ignite. I had a fire burning inside me, someplace, and I was now able to share it. I was brave. I was capable of doing, leading, learning—everything—for in spite of my affinity for the quiet, stable earth and my former fear of passionate, wild fire, I finally had lit a flame.

Celery

I cover my pale green walls with posters—
Phantom of the Opera
Sweeney Todd
The Joker
(and perhaps ironically)—
Peace—
because the color is not like me.

I am not faint.
I am not boring.
I am not weak.

Now I yearn to paint each wall a different shade,
represent the fragments of me:
Dark red, my passion,
Ocean blue, my dreams,
Chocolate brown, my comfort,
Pure purple, my soul.

But when I moved in,
I wanted it painted pale green.
Pale green for a pale girl,
distillation of her former self,
pale pitiful shade,
yearning to scream.

And I could scorn my former self,
embrace our alienation.
I could paint over the green
with fresher, newer hues,
colors that have no problem shouting out.

Or I could cover it with pieces
of who I am now,
of what I love now,
but still let that green peek out.
I don't want to forget it.
I don't want to forget her,
the girl I used to be.

And I know that green is the color
of growth.

Epiphany

BY THE TIME I graduated from YWFLA and completed my sophomore year of high school, it had been two years since my dad's death. I found myself deeply amazed at the growth I'd experienced and the pain and turmoil my family and I had overcome. I thought of myself two years earlier, a freshman just starting at SCPA. I was broken by my dad's death, frightened to be in an entirely new environment, and unkind to myself. Now, though I continued to miss my dad very much, I no longer felt a constant aching in my heart. I had found my place at SCPA, flourished in my art, and discovered a wonderful new set of friends, as well as maintained a connection with old ones. I had discovered new parts of my personality and learned to love myself. Like my father had told me to do so many times, I had finally learned to keep my head up.

By the time I headed out to California that summer, I felt eons away from the person I'd been the last time I'd touched down on the California terrain. Back then, I'd been an uncertain girl, caught in a flux of indecision, befuddled by the vicissitude of life. Now, I was a mostly happy girl, enjoying my ever-growing friendship with Avery and cherishing my place in our community of friends. When my Aunt Erin picked me up at the airport, she told me I seemed like an entirely different person.

I enjoyed a relaxing visit in California, spending time with my Aunt Erin, Aunt Kerry, and Aunt Trish. At one point, we all gathered at my Aunt Kerry's house for dinner, and my Aunt Chris and Roger, who were also vacationing at the time, were included. It was a rare occasion where my life and family at home intersected with my life and family in California. Amid my aunts, uncles, and cousins, and thinking of all my friends at home, I felt deeply aware of the abundance of my life for the first time in a while.

It was also during that trip that, one night while researching religion, I discovered I was an atheist. Atheism had always sounded like a cold, scary realm that I would never quite bring myself to: "Well, I'm not a Christian, but I do believe in God." But the more I considered it, I didn't think I did. I didn't think there was any greater being controlling human existence, caring about what we did or didn't do. I hadn't for a while. Yet a spiritless existence seemed empty to me, and I did believe that, somehow, my parents were still around, even if they weren't your archetypal angels in a cloudy, perfect heaven. It was a difficult paradox to explain, and one I still don't completely understand. I guess it's fair to say that I believe in some greater energy or unity that bonds all living things together—something greater, more powerful, and more significant than humans. Some people call that thing God, but I don't because the term implies a personal quality to the energy, a deity with thoughts and emotions, and this was an idea I rejected. Whatever it is, it is bigger than us, beyond understanding by our limited consciousnesses, and not something to be praised, in my opinion, but simply acknowledged and respected.

After a bit of research, I became aware of the notion of theism—that is, the belief in a deity that controls and/or cares about human goings-on. And since I didn't believe in such a thing, I was technically an atheist. Bingo! It was like something finally clicked. Coming to atheism wasn't, as I'd previously envisioned, the result of long nights of thinking or a deeply tragic event. It was simple logic. And instead of feeling lost or pointless, I actually felt happy. From now on, I could do good things just for the sake of doing them. I didn't have to worry about being judged or being good enough. I felt miraculously free. And, contrary to general conceptions, I wasn't "angry" at God for "taking" my parents away so early. The way I saw it, no one controlled what had happened to me. It's just how things turned out, and there was certainly no one to blame.

However, because of my belief in some realm of mysticism, I began to refer to myself as a spiritual atheist: one who has a sense of spirituality, but rejects traditional theism. I suppose some people would call such an ideology a watered-down paradox, and in some ways, it is. But it worked for me, and I was happy to finally find a faith—or lack thereof—to call my own.

Instructions

Give up God. Stop thinking
that everything happens for a reason,
that you'll be rewarded for the good.
Stop wondering
if you'll be punished for the bad.
In fact,
give up good and bad,
mere objective perceptions.
Give up fairness, justice,
give up religion, the idea of holiness,

then give up guilt.
Be bad and don't apologize.
Be bad and be accountable,
but guiltless.
Be good and expect
no greater reward
than being, doing, feeling.
Give up living for a utopian, far-off future,
free of guarantee—

and take up living for living:
realize
there needn't be anything else.

Liberation

I MADE ANOTHER big discovery that summer. Though I'd had a lovely time visiting, I found myself wondering what was going on at home and missing everyone each day. That year, I didn't even consider staying in California. However unglamorous, I realized that, for now, Cincinnati was my home. I felt happy and excited to return.

On the last day of my visit, I was finally able to visit the ocean.

30 June 2008

Today was beautiful. Aunt Kerry drove me—just me and her— down to Los Angeles to Aunt Erin's house. We listened to Damien Rice and talked. The boys were supposed to come with us but ended up staying behind.

When we got to L.A., Aunt Erin had prepared a little birthday celebration for Aunt Kerry. It was belated but nice. Aunt Kerry was surprised and happy. We ate and talked.

That night I laid on the floor of the living room listening to my family have a passionate discussion about politics—so typical. Then we ate some chocolate cake for Aunt Kerry's birthday. Then we decided to walk down to the beach as the sun was setting.

I wanted to go because my other California objective was to, of course, swim in the ocean. During my visit, I'd been twice to a beach but hadn't swam either time, so I was a little frustrated. So we walked to the beach and took some pictures, and then Aunt Kerry and I walked down to the shore. On the way down, I had these fanciful little visions of me going into the water in spite of my clothes. But I didn't really think I would because the sun was setting and I thought the water would be cold.

But when we reached the shore, the sun was smiling before it disappeared behind the hills in the distance. There were a few people splashing in the water. The sand was bathed in the warm pinks and oranges of the sunset, and the light reflected off the water, and it looked warm. I left Aunt Kerry at the shore to see how warm the water was. It was perfect. And I knew I had to go in. I went back and wrapped Aunt Erin's shawl, which I'd had around my shoulders, around Aunt Kerry's and kicked off my flip-flops.

"I want to go in," I said.

"Do you think you can?"

"I think so."

Then I ran into the water. No hesitation. I just went in and when it was deep enough, I submerged my head, and my heart was singing. I was finally with it again, the water, the ocean, and it welcomed me. My dress billowed around me in the water. I didn't even bother to take my jewelry off. I raised my arms in the air because I was joyful.

Waves washed over me, and I was joyful. I turned around and waved at Aunt Kerry, and I was laughing, swimming, and soaking in the smell, the sensation. And soon Aunt Erin and Uncle Javi joined Aunt Kerry at the shore, and my family stood there watching me swim in my dress, free and happy. Javi took pictures.

At some point, I got out of the water, dress plastered to my body, hair dripping. I felt high. I stumbled about and felt so happy and complete and in-touch and couldn't stop smiling.

Aunt Erin was admiring me because I was brave for just plunging in, and I felt brave and beautiful.

I walked home dripping wet, and we were happy, and Aunt Kerry was happy and laughing, and I love her so much. She was very close to my mom. She lived with my parents when when my mom was pregnant with me and I was a baby, and I love to be with her. We can talk for hours. And we did.

We came back to Aunt Erin's, and I took a warm shower, and my skin felt so soft, and I felt relaxed and warm and perfect. Then Aunt Erin made me a cup of chamomile tea, and I put honey in it. When it was time for Aunt Kerry to leave I wanted to cry because I love her. We hugged three times, and I hoped hard that she would come home for Christmas with her sons.

After Aunt Kerry left, Aunt Erin and I went upstairs and put on my dad's CD, and I drank my tea and another cup afterward, and we played Scrabble. We both played a good game. At one point, Aunt

Erin's letters spelled "Cincy" and "me," and then, shortly after, mine spelled "Ohio." Cosmic much? Honest.

Aunt Erin cried a little when my dad sang "If I Can Dream," and I smiled when he talked about me on the CD, and I wondered what he would think if he saw me now. And while we played Scrabble, I talked about how I've changed, and she talked about how I've changed, and I said how happy and overwhelmingly ready I am. We talked about my dad and everything else. I told her I was an atheist now, and she reacted openly and warmly and said, "You're discovering all different parts of yourself out here," and it's so true.

We did tarot cards, and then we went to bed. And here I am now in this cozy little room in a twin bed that I love. And I've been wanting to write this journal entry since I got into the ocean, but more importantly, I was participating. I was loving my family and laughing and appreciating what characters they are and feeling high from plunging into the ocean and just smiling and drinking tea, and it was just beautiful.

I can't wait to see the pictures Javi took of me while I was in the ocean. Because that's perhaps the happiest and most peaceful and held I've felt. I swear. The happiness just coursed through me, bubbling over, and I laughed and smiled and loved.

Aunt Erin gave me one of my mother's rings. And Aunt Trish gave me one of my mother's nightgowns. And Aunt Kerry wanted to give me one of my mother's jackets, but there was no room. She'll continue to hold it for me.

Does this mean something? Do they think I'm ready now? I think I am.

I'm just changed. I'm so ready for something to happen, something to change. I feel so bold, so beautiful, so prepared.

And each of these wonderful women, my aunts, understands this so acutely, what I'm feeling, where I'm going. They love me so much, and I love them. I'm so grateful for them.

Not bad for my first day as an atheist. I've found more beauty in this day, not believing in any god, than I have in many of my other days as a theist.

I never want this day to end. But it will. I go home tomorrow. I get in at seven, and I'll be close to all the other people I love again. I'm ready to go home. I'm ready to start these changes, this life, this love.

This trip has been so full of growth and learning, much of which is just coming to fruition now. I'm fully realizing it. As I told Aunt Trish, this is the first time in my life I've ever been really aware of my own growth.

I think that's all. It barely touches the surface, but I can't say everything. I loved this day. I love my family. I love this existence.

Not Quite the End

IT'S HARD to know where to stop my story because, in truth, it is continuing, and I'm still growing and changing. It's also difficult to tie everything up neatly and without leaving any dangling questions. So here's where I am now as I write this.

I'm still at SCPA, almost a senior. I love it more each day and am so grateful to be in an environment that is creative, diverse, and liberal. I've had a few recent successes in writing and continue to develop my skills in narrative and poetry, as well as playwriting.

I continue to be an atheist, feminist, and vegetarian. I still don't consider myself a strict atheist, however. I still believe there is something ethereal inside each one of us and some greater connection among every living thing.

My relationship with my Aunt Chris has improved; my relationships with my California aunts, friends from West Chester, Avery, Monique, my dad's side of the family, and my new friends from SCPA are still going strong. I've lost track of a few people along my way, but I still wish everyone who has been in my life the best.

I still think of my dad often, of course, and miss him, though not semi-constantly, as I once did. At some point recently, I learned to stop living in the past, in a state of constant regret, anguish, and what-ifs. I've learned to draw happiness and love from the people in my life now, though my dad will always be in my heart, as will my mother. My parents planted the seed of my potential seventeen years ago. It's my responsibility now to make sure that it flourishes, whether or not they are here to see it grow and blossom. I'm not sure if they are or not, if life after death is just a pleasant pipe dream or if it's reality. But in my heart, I have two angels following me, watching me as I go.

Postscript

Football Game

Sitting in the stands,
just watching football players
be walked down the field
by their parents.
How proud those parent seem
to parade their strong boys
in front of the crowd.
Some boys hold their mother's hand,
I notice,
pointing it out.
She is quiet for a moment.

Does that ever make you sad?—
her voice
so quiet
against the contrast
of the noisy high school fans.
What?

I ask, not sure what she means.
Does that ever make you sad?—
again, as if I hadn't heard her.
I follow her gaze
and understand
but before I can answer:
If you ever need a parent
to walk you down some aisle
        I'll do it.
I smile.
The players keep walking.
Thanks.

Home Videos

When I watch old home movies
I can see into a world
that is far, far away
and I was hardly even part of.

I hear the laughter of my mother
and the smiling face of my father.
And I see them happy together
and me in the middle of it all.

I see the faces of aunts and uncles
long passed away,
living happily in that captured moment
unaware of what will happen someday.

Me: I'm unaware as well.
The grinning, chubby baby
sitting on my parents' laps.
I don't know they'll both be gone within years.

Eventually the tape comes to an end.
The recorder must have thought,
"They won't care about seeing that,"
when it's the only thing really worth seeing.

The happiness becomes,
once more, a thing of the past.
There's but one thing to do:
rewind the tape and watch it again.

Book Club Discussion Questions for CHELSEY

1. *CHELSEY* includes some of the author's poetry and other writing she created in the aftermath of her father's murder. In what ways do you think writing helped Chelsey cope with her grief?

2. Have you ever suffered a loss like the death of a parent or loved one? In what ways was your experience of mourning and grief similar to Chelsey's? How was it different?

3. After her father's death, Chelsey's life is uprooted again, as she loses her childhood home and has to figure out where she wants to live and go to school. What other challenges do you think Chelsey faced in redefining her day-to-day reality?

4. The author includes a number of poems in her book. How does the poetry feel different from the rest of her writing? Does it convey her emotions or experiences differently? In what ways?

5. While the focus of *CHELSEY* is on loss and recovery, the author also tells a parallel story—that of her search for a

religion or spiritual framework that feels like a fit. Why do you think this search for meaning is so important to Chelsey?

6. Do you think being brought up in a certain faith makes one more or less likely to want to explore other religions? Have you ever embarked on a personal quest to find spiritual meaning in your life? What did you discover about yourself?

7. Have you ever experienced something that seemed too overwhelming and horrific that, at the time, you questioned whether or not you would survive it? How did you get through that difficult time? What surprised you most about your recovery? Has it continued to affect you today? If so, how?

8. The author writes about her relationship with the ocean throughout the book. What do you think the ocean might symbolize for Chelsey in her personal journey?

9. What do you think was a pivotal moment in Chelsey's story where she realized she would survive her loss and would ultimately be okay?